WHAT
to say
and do
WHEN...

Appropriate Responses for
Every Situation

Jeri-Lynn Johnson

SILVERLEAF
PRESS

CONTENTS

INTRODUCTION

*W*e have all said something that we later regretted, often thinking of the perfect response very shortly after recognizing our blunder. This book is designed to allow you the opportunity to prepare for a myriad of situations so that when the time inevitably arises, you can handle the incident with poise, delicacy, and tact.

Often, when we say the wrong thing in any given situation, it is because we were unprepared for the situation at hand. Being caught off guard, we commit a social faux pas and our comment can, depending upon the gravity of the circumstances, become a relationship killer.

Bear in mind that not every one of the situations outlined throughout this book will apply to your current circle of family and friends. Nevertheless, many of these situations will arise for someone of your acquaintance at some time in your life.

If you don't read anything else, read General Guidelines. They provide valuable information that can be adapted to virtually any situation and are an easy reference or refresher course when you need help—fast.

This manual is meant to be your own *personal* guide to help your friends and family through whatever situation may arise in their lives. That is why we've added a place for you to make your own notes at the end of each chapter to reflect what *you* would do for your particular friends or family members. Remember, there is no "one-size-fits-all" approach when dealing with the trials and triumphs of unique individuals.

GENERAL GUIDELINES

·····························

to Help Friends Who Are Going through Adversity

"If there is anything I can do to help, please call me."

That's your idea of help? Oh, please. That phrase is probably the single most useless thing you can say. Even if it's sincere, it accomplishes nothing except making you feel like you did something when in fact you did nothing.

I've said it myself hundreds of times and genuinely meant it, but it wasn't until I needed help that I realized what a hollow phrase it is. Can you really imagine your grief-stricken friend saying, "Oh, yes, as a matter of fact I do need help. My house is a mess. Can you be here at eight o'clock tomorrow morning to clean it up for the funeral?" That is simply not going to happen. Often when we are in need of help, we silently wish somebody would see what we need and offer assistance. When they don't, we just dig in and do it ourselves or do without.

We all want to help our friends. We want to share their good times and be a support in times of adversity. One phrase that I have heard frequently throughout my life has been, "I want to help, but I don't know what to do." You will find specific things to do for a variety of situations throughout this book, but there are some general things that can be said for almost any situation. Consult the suggestions below:

1. Show your love. (Visit http://hometown.aol.com/jeri10/Anytime.html for 50 things you can do for anyone, anytime.)

2. Be supportive. Nod your head in agreement. Say things like "Good for you," "You did the right thing," "I'm proud of the way you are handling this," "I couldn't have been so strong," etc.

3. Be there—not just during the crisis, but for the long haul.

4. The most important thing you can do for your friend is to *listen*. Whether your friend has good news to share or is in the middle of a crisis, your friend wants and needs to talk about it. In crisis situations, it is particularly critical that your friend be allowed to talk about what has happened.

    There are three steps to getting through crisis. The person in crisis needs to:

    a) Talk about what happened.

    b) Talk about how he or she feels about what happened.

    c) Talk about what he or she plans to do about what happened.
    Notice I said: talk, talk, talk. This should remind you that your role as

a friend is to listen, listen, listen. God gave you two ears and one mouth. You need to use them proportionately.

5. Are you sick and tired of hearing the same thing over and over again? Have you been avoiding your friend because of it? Think about how you would feel if your friends were abandoning you in your time of need.

6. Visit. Do your visits leave you drained and depressed? Visit anyway.

7. Doing something, even if it is not perfect, is better than doing nothing. The old adage "It's the thought that counts" is true. The smallest act of kindness is worth far more than the noblest intention. People will appreciate any act of kindness and they will love you for it.

8. What people really want is just to know that someone cares. Your role is not to solve your friends' problems. What is needed from you is a sympathetic ear and small acts of kindness.

9. Your friend would like to hear how well she is doing. Tell her.

10. Put yourself in the other person's shoes and think of what you might need if it were you. You'll be surprised at your own creativity.

11. Books make excellent gifts. You might read through them quickly to be sure the content is suitable for the situation.

12. The more you know about what your friend is going through, the better you will be equipped to help. Do a little research on the web.

The important thing to remember is that everyone responds to tragedy in unique ways. What works for one person doesn't necessarily work for another. For instance, when my mother is in the hospital, she doesn't want anyone to visit her—not even her own children. She feels vulnerable in her weakened state and would prefer for people to ignore her ailment altogether. Conversely, I have a friend who would never speak to me again if I didn't visit her in the hospital, and she expects flowers and balloons to boot. To her, the friends that are there for you in times of crisis are the only friends worth having. And she keeps track of those who are absent and distances herself from them in the future.

There is not one right approach that works for everyone. When in doubt, ask. Jot down your friends' preferences as you become aware of them so when they need help, you'll know what to do.

GENERAL GUIDELINES
· ·

for Building and
Maintaining Friendships

$\mathcal{B}$e the type of friend you would want to have.

1. Take genuine interest in the other person.

2. Build them up and make them feel good about themselves.

3. Help them to be the type of person they want to be.

4. Don't pressure them to do things they don't want to do.

5. Don't expect them to change.

6. Love them unconditionally.

7. Take interest in their lives, their hopes, dreams, children, and hobbies.

8. Be approachable.

9. Be there in times of trial and triumph.

10. Be supportive.

11. Be sincere.

12. Anticipate their needs.

13. Be charitable.

14. Be kind.

15. Don't be jealous of the time they spend away from you.

16. Make time for them.

17. Be honest (but not unnecessarily so).

18. Don't just look for what you can get out of the relationship.

19. Be willing to give as well as to take.

20. Be selfless.

21. Give sincere compliments.

22. Say you're sorry (and mean it).

23. Call them up just to ask how they are doing.

24. Don't borrow money.

Would you like to know how to build and maintain your marriage? Read the above again!

WHAT TO SAY AND DO WHEN...

WHAT TO DO WHEN AN ACCIDENT CHANGES A LOVED ONE'S LIFE

*O*ur love for you will not change. You are the same person you have always been and we are able to see through the scars." "Despite what you may think, we don't love you because you are beautiful. We love you for the person you are inside, and you are still that person. People who love and care about you don't see the scars."

A burn victim will have to learn to deal with the reactions of others to him, the stares, the people pointing and whispering and knowing that he is the reason for it. Encourage him to develop a sense a humor about his condition. If he can make fun of himself ("I'm not just another pretty face"), it will put others at ease. If he were a serious person, he may not be amused when others joke with him. He may, in fact, be quite offended. You have to know the victim's personality in order to know how to interact with him.

The very best thing you can do, as always, is listen. It is critical that he be able to express his feelings, good and bad. Your advice, in response, is most likely not needed nor desired. He just wants a sympathetic ear.

Let the person direct the course of the conversation. Some need to vent their pain, anger, and frustration, while others want distraction from their daily worries. Those who have numerous visits often tire of detailing their pain with each new arrival. Allow them to talk about the trivial and mundane, such as sports, celebrity gossip, or another guilty pleasure. However, do not try to divert the topic from the person's afflictions if he is willing or even desirous to discuss them. Nothing appears more heartless to a person in distress than the friend who enters the hospital talking incessantly about the Super Bowl when the patient brings up his pain. While your intentions might be to deflect his attention and bring him solace, it may come across as tactless, insensitive, and callous.

In cases of blindness, limb loss, and paralysis, the person will need a lot of support from you and all of his or her friends since everything must be relearned. They, and you, will have to be very patient during this process.

The person needs to find meaning in his or her life. Help the person to do this. Assign specific tasks to perform. Do not be condescending or treat the person like a child. Remember that it is extremely difficult for a formerly self-reliant individual to accept the dependency of his new situation. Expect frustration and despair. Assure him that these goals can be achieved. Encourage the person to do things for himself, but don't push. In the beginning, help with that for which he asks. After you have assisted several times, suggest it be tried solo, with you standing by to help achieve the goal. Praise all accomplishments.

Visit often, if that is acceptable to your friend. While many people appreciate the companionship, others feel embarrassed by their newly debilitating circumstances. Some individuals need time to regain a modicum of self-sufficiency and independence *before* they receive visitors, especially if their accident requires that they relearn many simple daily tasks. Make sure to inquire about the patient's desire for company. Does he want only immediate family members? Family and close friends? The more the merrier?

Everyone gets a lot of attention the first few months, but the cards, letters, and visits taper off. Friends tend to go on with their lives and the patient's good spirits start to plummet. Mark your calendar to remind you to call or visit once a month. If everyone did that, the person would have something to look forward to. If you don't know what to say, bring a friend or group who can carry the conversation.

What would I want someone to do for me if I were in this situation?

_____

_____

NOTES:

_____

_____

_____

_____

WHAT TO DO WHEN YOU WITNESS AN ACCIDENT OR A CRIME IN PROGRESS

*I*f you witness an accident or crime, don't assume someone else will report it. *Always* call 911. It is better to have several people report the same incident than for everyone to remain silent trusting that someone else will do something. Do not question whether the severity of the accident warrants 911 intervention; make the call and allow the operator to make that determination.

In the case of an accident, call 911. Depending upon the severity of the accident, someone's life may depend upon a prompt response from the appropriate department. Write down the license numbers of people involved (especially if they are fleeing the scene). Get a clear impression in your mind of what happened and whom you think was at fault. If the accident is on a major freeway, do not stop. You will only contribute to the traffic congestion, impede the emergency vehicle's response, and endanger your own life. The last thing you want to do is necessitate another 911 call on your behalf. If you choose to stop, be aware of your surroundings. Is there leaking fuel, smashed glass, or exposed power lines? If you do not stop, give the 911 operator your telephone number and tell her that you witnessed the accident but you are unable to stay. (If it is a bad accident with injuries and you have children in your car, you might not want to stop and subject them to the scene.) The police may wish to contact you about your statement.

If you witness a crime, resist the impulse to intercede. If the aggressor has a weapon, you could be endangering yourself before help can be notified. Always call 911 first. Then, if you want to help the victim, yell from a distance and call attention to yourself. Often, violence is abated when the aggressor is aware that his crime is being witnessed and that the police are on their way. Do not enter the proximity of the crime scene, but take in as many details as you can about the perpetrator. His approximate age, height, weight, clothing, hair color, body piercings, tattoos, or other distinguishing features may prove indispensable in prosecuting and convicting the criminal. Also note what is being said, types of weapons involved, vehicles involved, and direction of travel if the perpetrator flees the scene. Do not talk with anyone else about what you have seen because your testimony will be considered "corrupted" by the comparison with others' accounts and, therefore, unreliable. When it is safe to do so, write down exactly what you saw while you still have a vivid recollection of events.

What to Do If You Are the Victim of a Crime

If you are the victim of a robbery, comply. Credit cards can be cancelled, IDs can be replaced, and money can always be earned. Material objects or possessions are not worth risking serious injury or even death. If the robbery takes place in public, such as at a place of business, a crowded park, or a mall, do not talk about the event with other witnesses. The police will require your testimony free from the interpolations and influence of other witnesses.

If you arrive at your home or business and see a broken window or other evidence of a forced entry, do not enter the building. Call 911 immediately and find a safe location to await law enforcement.

Rape victims *must* resist the impulse to shower. You will wash away vital evidence that could be key in convicting your attacker. If you do not wish to call 911 (for fear of a male response) go to the hospital where you can receive proper medical care and receive the aid of nurses trained to respond to victims of rape. Be aware that if you call 911 and a male officer responds, you may request a female deputy. Be sure to preserve untouched any physical evidence at the scene (clothing, alcohol containers, condoms, anything that could possibly provide fingerprints, hair samples, or bodily fluids).

As is the case with any type of physical assault, many question whether or not they should attempt to fight back. Unfortunately, there is no right or wrong answer. Many potential victims have escaped harm by fighting their aggressors and running away. Conversely, others have sustained brutal beatings and even permanent injuries or disfiguration by fighting back. If you are being attacked and wish to fight back, keep these tips in mind:

a) Analyze the height, weight, and build of your attacker. Can you legitimately repel someone of his build?

b) If you choose to fight, are you willing to commit? The most vulnerable points of attack are the eyes, groin, throat, instep, and nose. A simple knee to the groin will only buy you so much time and could result in the increased fury of your assailant. Gauging out a person's eyes might prove invaluable for your escape, but are you willing and capable of doing so?

In any event, be the best witness you can be. Take a detailed note of clothing, physical description, what was said, types of weapons displayed, vehicles involved, and direction of travel.

NOTES:

WHAT TO DO WHEN YOUR LOVED ONE IS DEALING WITH AN ADDICTION

*Y*our role as a friend to someone with any kind of addiction is to make your friend accountable for his actions. Set goals and encourage him to accomplish them.

Drugs and/or Alcohol

As a general rule, don't confront the person when he is high or drunk. Wait until the next day. Tell him what you observed and the kinds of problems it created. Describe your feelings. Remain calm. Set limits on what you will tolerate. He will most likely deny that he has a problem; denial is one of the symptoms. Drop it, but call it to his attention every time it happens, until he finally admits he has a problem. Successful treatment and recovery require a long-term commitment.

What You Can Do

Contact your local treatment facility. They have trained counselors who can coach you on how to plan an "intervention."

When you go out together socially, don't order alcohol. Suggest things to do together that have no association with alcohol. Go to a movie, go to a gym class, cooking class, oil painting class, etc. Invite them to your church activities. Get them involved in a charity organization. Go to places for lunch or dinner that don't serve alcohol.

Don't cover up their behavior.

Don't hide the full impact of their behavior from the user.

Don't take over the user's responsibilities.

Don't rationalize the drug as a benefit for the user.

Don't cooperate by buying the drug.

Don't be deceived. All illegal drugs are detrimental to one's health. They are mind-altering, behavior-altering, and potentially deadly. Moreover, they are illegal. It is a crime to even hold them in one's possession. Don't ignore the potential risk your friend or loved one is incurring.

According to a *Primetime* segment on marijuana that aired March 19, 1997, there are some things you should know about the marijuana on the streets today. It is four times stronger than the "weed" available in the 1960s. Daily use interferes with short-term memory. One to three uses a day equals five times as many cigarettes and puts you at a high risk for cancer. It is not only addictive (100,000 people enter treatment centers every year), but it is also a "gateway" to other drugs. Sixty-five percent of users move on to cocaine, acid, or other drugs.

Cocaine affects the brain (behavioral problems, stroke, seizures, or death), the heart (heart attack, death), the digestive system (liver damage), and the reproductive system (crack babies). Snorting cocaine causes problems with the mucous membranes in the nose. One of the worst consequences of injecting cocaine is the possibility of contracting AIDS from needle sharing.

Don't underestimate the power of the drug culture. Americans spend $40–50 billion (that's billion with a "B") on drugs every year. Three-fourths of that money is for cocaine.

How can you tell if someone is abusing drugs?

a) Secretive behavior

b) Mood swings

c) Anxiety and nervousness

d) Impulsive behavior

e) Change in friends

f) Weight loss

g) Neglect of appearance

h) Denial that a problem exists

What you can do for teens:

Pharming parties are a recent phenomenon among today's youth. The term refers to prescription pharmaceuticals being abused in unorthodox ways. Many youth who would never dream of using an illegal drug, see no harm in taking medications for which they do not carry prescriptions. When taken in conjunction with a myriad of meds (everything from Ambien to Zanax) the results can be both hallucinogenic and lethal. Teens need to be advised that *any* drug can be harmful if abused. Common drugs like Prozac and Ritalin are not meant to be snorted, injected, or used in abnormal dosages. Moreover, when household meds are taken in certain combinations, they are deadly. The danger of pharming is that kids feel that they are being "safe" by using prescriptive substances. Unfortunately, they rarely know the dosage or even the nature of the pills they are combining in search of their next high.

Help your child prepare a list of ways to "just say no," so she will be ready when the time comes. Keep lines of communication open. Talk to your kids about your concerns for them and their health. Let them know what you expect of them.

If your child is "drifting," try to steer her into finding a group where she can meet new friends who share their interests. Keep your kids busy. Suggest that they try out for a sport, join a club, pursue any interest they have. Too much idle time can lend itself to problems. Keep them so busy that they don't have time to hang out with the wrong crowd or experiment with harmful substances. Know your children's friends. Encourage your children to bring their friends over. When they are out, know whom they are with and what they are doing. Ask questions.

Positive self-esteem is another powerful tool in avoiding addictions.

One way to build self-esteem is to provide the child with opportunities to feel good about herself. Sign up to be a "buddy" at the Special Olympics in your area and bring your teen. She will learn how to interact with the handicapped and feel good about herself. Look for ways to include your teen in any service projects you do.

Home drug tests are available. If a teen has been suspended from school for drug use, the principal should ask for periodic drug tests to be submitted to his office (by having the principal ask for the test, it takes the strain off the parent/child relationship).

What would I want someone to do for me if I were in this situation?

_____

_____

NOTES:

_____

_____

Gambling

If you haven't already read the preceding section "Drugs and/or Alcohol," read it now. It applies here as well, especially the denial part. Men don't seem to think there is anything wrong with gambling, but it can be as damaging to relationships as drugs and alcohol. Money that should be going toward the family is being squandered irresponsibly. Do a quick search on the Internet on gambling addiction and you will see very quickly how serious this addiction can be.

Encourage the person to call Gamblers Anonymous or seek professional counseling.

How can you tell if a person has a gambling problem?

a) Has he lost time from work in order to gamble?

b) Does he think constantly of gambling and ways to get gambling money?

c) Does he gamble until all the money is gone?

d) Does he lie to hide his gambling activity?

e) Does he rely on friends to bail him out of debt?

f) Has he tried to quit and can't?

A "yes" to any one of these questions indicates a problem with gambling. The person needs to seek professional help.

When someone is in this kind of trouble, whether it be gambling, shopping, or any number of obsessive behaviors, that person needs help.

What You Can Do

1. Don't support the habit by lending money.

2. Don't go to places where the person will be tempted to spend money on the habit. Suggest alternative activities. If your friend likes to bet with golf partners, don't suggest golf. Go to a movie. Go out to dinner. Go to the beach. Get involved in a charitable organization.

3. Encourage the person to call Gamblers Anonymous or seek professional counseling.

What would I want someone to do for me if I were in this situation?

_____

_____

Notes:

_____

_____

Pornography

As with gambling, many men don't believe that there is a problem in looking at pornography. Many truly believe that simply all men look at pornography. They are wrong. There are men who value their relationship with their wives and don't want to pollute their minds with things that can be damaging to their relationship. Contrary to what they may think, porn is not harmless voyeurism. It involves a dangerous progression. Those who view it often find themselves spending more and more time looking and even begin contacting people and exchanging personal information.

If a man asks, "Why is my wife so upset about it? What's it to her?" Your answer should be, "She is no longer the focus of your attention. Instead, you have traded in a living, breathing, loving mate for an inanimate image on a piece of paper or video. From the standpoint of intimacy, you left the marriage. What loving wife wouldn't be upset about that?"

"Your wife is not expressing her expectation of you nearly as much as she is her needs. She needs you to adore her, to protect her, to think of her as the only woman in the world. Her needs of intimacy and genuine compassion can never be met so long as she is on the back burner and other people whom you do not even know are placed ahead of her. She cannot be fulfilled when half of the marriage has departed, and that is exactly what any married pornography addict has allowed to happen."

He says he is not addicted. Okay. Challenge him to stop. See how long he can go. If he's honest, he will see that he has a problem. Twelve step programs can help. But in the end, it is he who has to commit to stopping his behavior.

How would I handle it?

_____

_____

NOTES:

_____

_____

HOW DO YOU GET YOUR ADULT CHILDREN TO MOVE OUT OF YOUR HOUSE?

*O*rder them to stay! (Just kidding)

According to my husband, helping your children move on is quite easy. You simply tell them to "Go to the end of the driveway and turn left." (Then change the locks on your doors). That is obviously not practical—tempting, but not practical. So, joking aside, how do you get them out?

As tough as it may be to cut the proverbial apron strings, it's for your child's own good to push him out of the nest and force him to fend for himself.

If the young man is a good kid—going to school, working, and trying to save money for his future—try to be patient. It's a lot harder to make it in the rising cost of today's world.

I know people who started charging their son rent, figuring if he had to pay rent, he'd rather be on his own, with his friends. It didn't work. He never paid it. He got six months behind in the rent and when his parents challenged him, his answer was, "So sue me." (I think in this case, if I were his mom, I would have changed the locks).

If he is no longer going to school and is still living at home, ask him to move out. Help him find a job, pay his first month's rent, set up his apartment, and tell him he is now on his own. Don't give him any money. As long as you keep bailing him out, he has no incentive to change. Remind yourself that you are only doing your child a disservice by enabling his dependence and irresponsibility.

OTHER IDEAS:

_____

_____

_____

_____

HOW CAN I CARE FOR MY AGING PARENTS?

*A*t least 22.4 million Americans are caring for aging parents at any one time. One of the biggest roadblocks in helping aging parents is that most insist they don't need or want help. It is often better to take baby steps toward the ultimate solution. Start by having someone come into the person's home to clean, then prepare meals. The next step would be to move to an assisted-living situation. When the person becomes bed-ridden, or disoriented, it's time to move to a nursing home.

As long as the person is living in his or her own home, it is wise to have the phone number of a neighbor. If you suspect things might be deteriorating, check with the neighbor. Be sure the neighbor has your telephone number and instruct the neighbor to call you if he or she notices anything out of the ordinary.

What You Can Do

1. Visit. Bring your children with you (most enjoy seeing young people).

2. Listen to the person, even if it's the same story over and over.

3. Take the person for a ride.

4. Surprise the person with a "This is your life" party.

5. Help the person write his or her life history or tape record it.

6. Write letters for the person if he or she is unable to write.

7. Read if the person's vision is failing.

8. Have a hearing device attached to the person's phone if hearing is impaired.

9. Have a luncheon or tea party for the person and a few of his or her friends.

10. Have nutritious meals brought in (check to see if there is a "Meals on Wheels" in your area).

Is the person's diet restricted? If on a soft diet and you'd like to bring a treat, bring soup or a pudding.

Watch for signs of depression and if it lasts longer than two weeks, notify the person's doctor.

What would I want my family and friends to do for me when I'm old?

_____

_____

WHAT TO DO FOR ANNIVERSARIES

*H*ere is a list of traditional and modern gift ideas:

Traditional	Modern
1st Paper	Clock
2nd Cotton	China
3rd Leather	Crystal
4th Flowers	Appliances

5th Wood	Silverware
6th Candy	Wood
7th Copper	Desk Set
8th Bronze	Linens
9th Pottery	Leather
10th Aluminum	Diamond Jewelry
15th Crystal	Watch
20th China	Platinum
25th Silver	Silver
30th Pearls	Diamonds
35th Coral	Jade
40th Ruby	Ruby
45th Sapphire	Sapphire
50th Gold	Gold

Don't feel confined to this list. Draw from your own personal experiences. Make a scrapbook of favorite times together, create a collage of meaningful photos, make reservations for your anniversary dinner at the restaurant where you became engaged.

If you are a young couple hearing of an older couple's anniversary, ask them what the secret of success is to a long marriage. You might learn something.

The White House will send a greeting to couples who are celebrating their 50th (and subsequent) wedding anniversary. Go online to www.white-house.gov or send your request, including the name and address of the recipients, the exact date of the anniversary and your name and phone number, so that it is received at least six weeks before the anniversary date, to:

The White House
Attn: Greetings Office
Washington, D.C. 20502–0039

MY IDEAS:

_____

_____

WHAT TO DO FOR AN 80TH BIRTHDAY

*R*eaching the age of eighty is a milestone and should be celebrated. What to plan has a lot to do with the health of the person.

It doesn't really matter what you do as long as you do something. Have a family reunion and have everyone make an effort to be there. Collect photos from every family and make a scrapbook. Make sure everyone makes a point to visit before the year is out. The person just wants to know that people care.

If the person is in a rest home, call every family and make sure they all send a card.

When you sing happy birthday, do you add "and many more"? Sure, why not—unless they are terminally ill.

The White House will send a greeting to individuals 80 years of age and above. It must be received at least six weeks before the event. Go online to www.whitehouse.gov or mail your request (including name and address of honoree, exact date of birthday, and your name and phone number) to:

The White House
Attn: Greetings Office
Washington, D.C. 20502

MY IDEAS:

_____

_____

WHAT TO DO WHEN YOUR CHILD WALKS IN DURING AN ARGUMENT

*I*f there is yelling going on, it should stop immediately. Say, "Sorry, we just got carried away. It's not as bad as it looked. Sometimes when we don't think the other person understands how we feel about something, we think if we talk louder they'll understand. Silly isn't it?"

If you think you can resolve the issue calmly, do so. That will teach your child that arguments can be resolved without stomping out and slamming doors. If not, say to your spouse as calmly as possible, "Let's talk about this later when we've both calmed down."

Somehow we've gotten the idea that whoever yells the loudest wins. Unfortunately, when the yelling starts, you both lose because the relationship has gone haywire. Try to work on resolving your issues without raising your voices. When one starts, the other should say, "You don't have to yell. I'm in the room."

Explain to your child that, while we sometimes have differences of opinion, it does not change our love for one another. People sometimes fight and disagree, but we still love each other unconditionally, even in the hard times. If your argument was handled in an inappropriate fashion, use the situation as a teaching moment. Explain how your conduct could have been improved. Let your child know that sometimes even mommies and daddies make mistakes. (If your child is a teen, he has undoubtedly already discovered this.) Then be sure to work on controlling your temper. Your actions will speak much louder than any verbal lessons you wish to teach your children.

How would I handle this situation?

_____

_____

NOTES:

_____

_____

WHAT TO DO WHEN YOU NEED HELP ASKING FOR HELP

*W*hat if *you* are the one who needs help? How can you get your friends to help you?

1. When your friends say, "If you need anything, call me," your reply should

be something like this: "Thank you, I will. Is there anything in particular you would like to do? You know, so I can call you if I need that
kind of help." or "Thank you, I will. What kinds of things would you
like me to call you for?" or "Thank you, I will!" (Then do.)

2. When the time comes that you really need some help, be daring. Pick
   up the phone and say, "Well, you said if I ever needed anything to give
   you a call, I hope you meant it because I really need. . . ."

3. If you just can't bring yourself to ask for help, drop some not so sub-
   tle hints like: "I just can't seem to get organized. My laundry is piled
   so high I get depressed looking at it." If your friend doesn't pick up on
   that, add: "I wish I had a magic wand to make it disappear." If she still
   doesn't volunteer, add: "You don't know of anyone who would come in
   and do laundry do you?" If she still doesn't volunteer, try someone else,
   or, if you can, hire someone to come in and do it for you.

A special note to women readers: do not become angry or embittered
towards your friends if they fail to pick up on a veiled plea for help. We sometimes expect others to read through our subtleties and immediately perceive
our needs. This is not always the case. Many a well-meaning friend would, in
fact, be happy to do our laundry if we asked her outright. But often our friends
are afraid of being presumptuous. Don't assume that your friends will perceive the needs that you are afraid to vocalize. Alluding to a need *is not* the
same as asking for help.

*Is there anything I need help with right now? How can/would I ask people to help
me?*

WHAT TO SAY WHEN A FRIEND OR RELATIVE
ASKS TO BORROW MONEY

*M*y grandfather told me never to lend money to friends or relatives. We've all heard that, but how can you tell a friend or relative no? Our friends and family are the people we most want to be able to help!

The biggest problem with lending money to a friend is that you end up losing the friend.

They feel embarrassed when they can't pay you back, so they avoid you. You feel angry that they haven't even made an attempt to pay you back so you lose respect for them. You feel that their negligence is a sign of disrespect and that they are taking advantage of your friendship. It's a lose-lose situation. If you don't lend them the money, you feel bad and they feel betrayed. So what do you do?

The bottom line is that friends and relatives often fail to pay you back. It isn't intentional, but when one has a myriad of debts, those neglected are often not the creditors or debt collectors. So, if you don't care about never seeing the money again, go ahead and "lend" them the money. But to avoid the animosity between friends, it is best to remove even the presumption of "loaning" it. It is best to give the money as a gift with absolutely no intention of being paid back. That way, the friend does not feel awkward in your presence and, if the person does pay back the loan, you will be pleasantly surprised.

If you can't afford to lose the money, you have to find a way out. Explain that your finances are tight right now. Offer to do everything in your means. Tell them you don't have the whole amount they are asking for but that if they will come up with half the money, you will give them the other half. (I haven't had one person take me up on that. They say okay, but never bring it up again).

What would I want someone to do for me if I were in this situation?

_____

_____

NOTES:

_____

_____

WHAT TO DO WHEN MEETING YOUR SPOUSE'S BOSS FOR THE FIRST TIME

*I*t is important to make a good impression. I've known men and women who didn't get promotions because their spouse wasn't up to fulfilling his or her role. If the promotion calls for the person to attend social functions which would require his or her spouse to be there and he or she is unsuitable to represent the image of the company, the person will be passed over for an employee whose spouse fits the image. With that in mind, dress appropriately, be well groomed, and shake the boss's hand like you are really happy to meet him. Look him in the eyes and smile.

Be aware that in today's society, gender lines are blurred. A male CEO may have different expectations than his female counterpart. Be willing and able to adapt.

"I'm glad to finally meet you."

Instead of saying, "I've heard so much about you." Tell him the things you've heard, "My husband told me you just returned from a buying trip in Japan, what was it like?" Or "I understand you recently won the club championship golf tournament at your club. Congratulations." Or mention anything you may have in common.

For women, be gracious. For men, be polite and humble. Remember that you are there to let your spouse shine. You are merely an accessory to his or her corporate image. Be cordial and friendly, but let your spouse dominate the conversation. Avoid enumerating the indispensable qualities of your spouse, requesting a raise, or complaining about the workplace.

Don't talk about yourself unless he asks. Try to get him talking about the company. Men love to talk about their business. You can ask how long he has been with the company. Ask where he worked before joining the company and where he lived before. Then back off. You don't want to be too chatty. There is nothing wrong with silence. It gives him a chance to excuse himself to speak to others. When it comes time to leave, make a point of saying goodbye and how nice it was to meet him.

How would I handle this situation?

_____

_____

NOTES:

_____

_____

HOW TO BREAK UP A RELATIONSHIP

*G*ently, but firmly.

Don't feed the person any lines: "It's not you, it's me" (translation: it *is* you and I want better). "My life is just so busy/complicated, I don't have time for a relationship" (translation: Oh, I have time for a relationship, but not with *you*). People see through those clichés.

On the other hand, it isn't necessary to be brutally honest either. There is no need to enumerate the person's faults or annoying habits (. . . Number 83: you have really bad coffee breath, Number 84 . . .)

Just say, "I really don't see any potential for this relationship long term. I think you are a great person and a good catch for some lucky person, but I just don't think that person is me."

The truth is, you may date a hundred people throughout the course of your life, but you will only marry one (hopefully). It's good to date a lot of different people to find out what you want, but once you know that this person isn't "the one," don't waste their time or yours. Especially if you're in your mid to late twenties and beyond, don't string a person along. Let them down gently and give them a chance at finding happiness with someone who is right for them.

NOTES:

_____

_____

WHAT TO DO WHEN YOUR CHILD IS BEING BULLIED

*I*f the child is being bullied at school, the incident(s) should be reported to the school.

The only time you should confront the parent(s) of the bully is when the attack takes place in the presence of parents of both the bully and the victim.

If you are at a party and your child is pushed to the ground by another child, you can pick your child up, tell the child who pushed, "No, you are not to push other children down, do you understand me?" If the child does it again, you can go to the bully's mom and say, "Excuse me, your child has just pushed my child down twice and I can't get him to stop. Would you mind having a little talk with him."

The best thing you can do if your child is being bullied is to try to explain to him that it is not his fault. People who bully have self-esteem problems. It is the bully who needs to be pitied. Listen to your child, comfort him. Don't tell him to punch the kid in the face. That usually doesn't solve anything. Tell your child that if he feels he wants to say something to the bully, he can say, "I feel sorry for you." But if the bully's friends are in earshot, that might trigger a punch.

It is better for your child just to avoid the bully. Tell your son not to walk around school alone, try to walk with other kids. He'll be less likely to be a target if he can't be singled out. Tell your child to report the incident to an adult (teacher, lunchroom supervisor, principal, etc.) and take along any witnesses to the event. If he is hesitant to do it, you report it. The school has to keep records, and if enough reports are made, they may assign someone to keep an eye on the bully.

If the parent of the bully contacts you and asks what has been going on, explain everything you know about the situation. Remain as calm as possible. Don't get angry.

If the parent of the bully gets angry, you have a pretty good idea how the kid became a bully.

Back in "my day," when parents were called by a teacher or another responsible adult about their child's behavior, the parents believed the person and disciplined their child. Today, parents immediately deny any possibility that their child could have been involved. They believe their children over the adults. Hello, why would we lie about such a thing? If you are the mom being called about your little angel, take another look. Be willing to accept the fact that your child is lying to you in order to avoid punishment. "It happened before I was born," should not get him off the hook. Assume he is guilty until proven innocent.

How would I react if my child were being bullied?

How would I react if it were my child that was the bully?

NOTES:

WHAT TO DO FOR A LOVED ONE WHO HAS BEEN DIAGNOSED WITH CANCER

*B*eing told you have cancer is a very scary thing. Most people associate cancer with death, so the diagnosis feels like a death sentence. One's life suddenly has limits.

Your job is to support your friend and encourage him to be optimistic. Cancer is curable and your need to focus on that. Don't talk about people you know who died of cancer. Talk about the people you know that survived cancer.

Don't avoid your friend because you don't know what to say. Just go for a short visit and let the other do the talking, or go with someone else—but go. What you can say is, "I'm here for you." Then be there. Listen. Let him express his fears.

If it turns out to be terminal, don't try to be an amateur psychologist, analyzing your friend's every comment and action. Your presence is more important than what you say.

Encourage him to make plans for his death, but remind him that he is alive now and to enjoy each day he has.

Cancer's warning signs:

- a change in bowel or bladder habits
- a sore that does not heal
- unusual bleeding or discharge
- thickening or lump in breast or elsewhere
- indigestion or difficulty in swallowing
- obvious change in wart or mole
- nagging cough or hoarseness

If you or a friend has any of the above, see your doctor.

Medical tests that could save your life:

1. Mammography: women ages 50–69 should be tested annually. Women under the age of 50 should consult with their doctor about the frequency of testing.

2. Pap Smear: all women under 65 who have been sexually active should be tested at least once every three years.

3. Stool for hidden blood: all men & women over 50 should be tested annually.

4. Sigmoidoscopy (an exam using a scope to view the rectum and the lower

part of the large intestine routinely used to screen for cancer): all men and women over 50 should be tested every 5 to 10 years.

What You Can Do

Be a sounding board for your friend. Listen to the person's concerns and fears and be a source of comfort, reassurance, and support. Provide as much normalcy to the person's life as possible.

Support whatever decisions the patient has made about treatment. If the person is unsure about courses of treatments, suggest that the patient seek a second opinion, contact the National Cancer Institute Information Service, and read as much information as is available.

Greet your friend or loved one saying, "You are really doing great." Or, "You look really good considering all you are going through. How do you do it?" It's a real spirit booster. Your friend needs all the encouragement you can muster. Don't trivialize their condition by saying things like, "Things could be worse," or "It's all for the best."

If your spouse has breast cancer, prostate cancer, or any other disfiguring surgery, reassure her/him that you don't think any less of them as a person. You will love that person regardless of how he or she looks after surgery. Your mate needs your emotional support.

Put your friend's name on a prayer list or do whatever else one does in your religion. One man I know said the most impressive thing anyone ever said to him was, "We pray for you every night." He said that really meant a lot to him because he knew they were a very religious family and he knew they were sincere.

Tell your friend how people are asking about him and wishing him well. Offer to drive your friend to his or her chemo treatments. Go out to lunch afterward. Bring in dinner for her family the day of her treatment. She probably won't feel like cooking or eating, but her family will appreciate it.

Bring bread or rolls or crackers. These seem to be something anyone can eat after therapy. It helps with the nausea. I used to like chicken noodle soup or a mug of hot milk. Fruits and vegetables are the hardest to eat. They are too acidic and just the thought of them will lower the cancer patient's mood.

What would I want someone to do for me if I were in this situation?

_____

_____

NOTES:

_____

_____

WHAT TO SAY TO CELEBRITIES

*I*f you know a famous person you probably know they feel used and abused. They have the same need we all have and that is to be respected as a person. The person they are, not the sideshow character the press portrays. They want and need a real life with real friends. A life where their personal opinions count. A life where people aren't friendly toward them just to get favors from them.

Don't let yourself become involved in setting people up. If someone wants you to approach the celebrity to appear at a function, you could say, "_____ gets so many of those kinds of requests. He has asked me not to get involved in his business. Let me give you his manager's telephone number. He is really the one to talk to. _____ would have to clear it with him anyway."

What if a celebrity moves next door? Should you go knock on their door and introduce yourself? Well, what would you do for anyone else who moved in? Are you the type who knocks on their door? Do exactly what you would for a stranger. Don't treat the celebrity any differently. Don't fall all over yourself trying to make friends, but don't ignore them either. Be yourself. Welcome them to the neighborhood.

What if you are in a restaurant and a celebrity comes in for dinner? Are you in the habit of walking up to strangers in a restaurant and introducing yourself? If not, don't do it to the celebrity.

Famous people do like to be acknowledged but all that is needed is a big smile of recognition and maybe a thumbs-up, if that is your style. But please don't try to intrude on their privacy.

How would you like it if every time you went out to dinner, you had everyone in the restaurant come up to you and try to talk to you, or ask you for an autograph, or ask to be photographed with you. It would get old very quickly.

If you find yourself in a situation where it is appropriate to speak, speak to them like you would anyone else. If you are alone in an elevator together or seated next to him/her on an airplane you might say, "Fancy meeting you here. I really admire your work." Then let the celebrity decide whether he/she wishes to continue the conversation.

Wives of famous men and husbands of famous women often feel used by people. People try to make friends with them in order to get access to their spouse. Imagine what that would do to your self-esteem. They want to be recognized, loved, and appreciated for their own contributions and not constantly in the shadow of their famous other half. The same goes for children of celebrities.

Celebrities and their families get pretty good at spotting users. Back off.

What I would say (no more than one sentence):

_____

WHAT DO YOU DO WHEN YOU DISCOVER THAT YOUR FRIEND'S HUSBAND IS CHEATING ON HER?

*Y*ou have to risk the chance of the old proverbial "shoot the messenger" response.

Your friendship may suffer as a result of you telling your friend. But in this day and age, with AIDS and other dangerous STDs, your silence could endanger your friend's health, and possibly her life. You have to tell her.

First, be absolutely sure that the spouse is, in fact, cheating. Do not tell your friend based on gossip or hearsay. Next, tell her how and what you know.

Be gentle. Try to imagine how you would feel to receive this news and act accordingly. Be supportive. She may yell at you, ignore you, accuse you of jealousy or lies. Do not respond with anger. ("I'm trying to do you a favor and you jump down my throat? Well I guess that's what I get for trying to be a good friend!") Instead, expect an outburst. Expect resentment or hostility. Remain calm and supportive. Explain how difficult it is to report such horrible news. Tell her the struggle you had deciding how to handle the situation, but that ultimately, you would want to be told if it were your husband. Give her time to adjust to the news. Offer your love and support regardless of how she chooses to deal with the situation. Do not offer suggestions as to what she should do. It is not your place to suggest divorce. Resist the urge to call him names like "schmuck," "louse," "jerk," etc. The husband will inevitably deny the accusations and may even conjure up a story implicating *your* bad motives ("Who told you? Oh she's been hitting on me a lot lately but I've told her I'm committed to you." "She just wants to split us up because her marriage is in pieces.") In the end, she may not believe you or, if she does, may still opt to remain with her husband. (If the latter proves true, you will be very grateful you said nothing to defame her spouse.) Respect her decision and try to be there for her if she needs a friend.

NOTES:

_____

_____

_____

_____

WHAT TO DO WHEN YOU START THINKING ABOUT CHEATING ON YOUR SPOUSE

*H*as that handsome prince you married turned into a frog? Unfortunately, there are very few happily-ever-after's. Marriage is a succession of highs and lows. Most of us will fall in and out of love over a dozen times before we reach the "'til death do us part" termination of the marital contract.

Remember the reasons you fell in love in the first place. Chances are, he hasn't changed very dramatically. That is very often the problem. If there is one thing we learn from *Madame Bovary,* it is that adultery often springs from boredom, monotony, or dissatisfaction with our lives. Other men begin to look more exciting. But before you start romanticizing about your life with someone else, remember that you will only be trading in one set of problems for another.

Benjamin Franklin said, "Keep your eyes wide open before marriage, and half shut afterwards." More often than not, the heinous blemishes you see in your spouse after many years are not new flaws. They are often the same "quirks" you tolerated or even found endearing at one time. Nevertheless, time can extinguish the flames of love and passion. Our lives become routine, boring. Do not wait for your partner to change the momentum of your marriage. Take ownership of your life and *be* the change you wish to see.

The only way you can make him treat you better is for you to treat him better. Every day say something kind to him. Reach out and hold his hand. Pat his leg. Look him in the eyes when you talk to him. Smile. Walk him to his car when he leaves. Wave goodbye. Fix a special dinner. Go for a walk together. See a movie together. Talk about things in your past that evoke fond memories. Talk about things you'd like to do in the future (travel? re-locate?). What will you do when you retire?

It's taken a long time to get where you are. It's going to take a long time to get it better. Be patient.

When you find yourself losing it, bite your tongue. Don't say anymore. Wait 24 hours before saying what's on your mind. Don't drag out everything he ever did to upset you. The past is past—forgive. Forget.

Do you want to think about divorce? Okay, think about it. But think about all of it. Think about how the children will react, not only to it, but to you for doing it. Think about how ugly people get over property settlements. Think about how you are going to feel when he remarries (and he will). Think about "dating" again, in this world. Think about trading all the faults you "know" for someone else's that you don't know. Think about holidays. Think about income taxes. Think about having to go back to work. Think about scaling down your lifestyle. Think about being alone. Think about being old and alone. Think about not being included by your friends anymore because you are not a "couple" anymore. You are the "odd man out." Think about your friends having to choose between you and your husband.

Don't dwell on the negative. You know the old saying: "Ulcers are not caused by what you eat, they're caused by what's eating you." When a negative thought comes into your head, immediately replace it with a positive thought.

Quit talking negatively about him to your friends. When they ask, simply say, "Things are looking up" and smile. Don't confide in male "friends."

Forming emotional bonds with members of the opposite sex while experiencing marital difficulties can be very risky.

Don't expect anyone else to make you happy. You are the only one who can make you happy. Do things that make you happy. Paint, take an art class, do community service, garden, take piano lessons, learn a new skill, read, do lunch, shop, visit friends, organize and teach a class, start collecting something, write a book, sew, research your ancestors, organize closets and drawers, etc.

And remember, you are not alone. You are not the only woman who has ever felt the way you do. Every woman feels that way from time to time. The question is, how much of the time—once a year, once a month, once a day, or hourly? Do not let yourself dwell upon these thoughts. They will be a self-fulfilling prophecy if you entertain them long enough.

Seek professional help. A marriage counselor can help you rekindle what's lost.

Who knows, you may be going through your mid-life crisis. If you are, don't leave your husband behind. Take him with you. (And then, hopefully, he'll take you with him through his.)

NOTES:

_____

_____

_____

_____

WHAT TO DO IF YOU SEE A CLASSMATE CHEATING ON A TEST

*C*heating has become an epidemic in this country and students are start-ing earlier and earlier.

College students can get copies of tests and final exams on the Internet. Students from a morning class will give a student in an afternoon class a copy of the test. Students use their cell phones to text each other during exams. There is no end to it.

It used to be a big no-no to blow the whistle on a cheating classmate. But when teachers grade on a curve, it really affects everyone's grades when even one person cheats. Moreover, the chances are that you are not the only person who witnessed the classmate cheating. As long as he gets away with it, other students may feel compelled to cheat in order to keep up their GPAs. Cheating can become an epidemic as other students feel the pressure to compete.

Rather than raise your hand in the middle of class to tell the teacher, it is better to stay after class and more discreetly tell what you saw. Your silence isn't serving anyone. As long as people continue to get away with it, they will continue to cheat.

How would I go about reporting a cheating incident?

_____

_____

_____

WHAT TO SAY WHEN YOUR FRIEND'S SON GETS INTO THE COLLEGE OF HIS CHOICE AND YOURS DOESN'T

*G*etting into the college of your choice is getting harder and harder these days. There are twice as many people applying than there were ten years ago. Even 4.0 students get declined.

There are a lot of things that are considered. The grade point is only one part of the equation. The school from which the student is applying is also considered. A 3.5 from School A might be more highly regarded than a 4.0 from School B. Then extra curricular activities are taken into account. If the college has a competitive sports team and the student is a superstar in that sport, he probably has a better chance of getting in than someone else with the same grade point.

When all is said and done, most kids end up at the college where they belong and will do the best in the end. If you are determined to have your child graduate from Harvard or Yale, they can always work toward transferring over in their junior year.

Be happy for your friend's son. It's okay to tell your friend that you wish your son had been accepted as well so they could continue to hang out.

What would I want someone to say to me if I were in this situation?

_____

_____

NOTES:

_____

HOW TO GIVE AND RECEIVE COMPLIMENTS

*I*t's easier to give than receive" applies to compliments as well. For some reason we tend to deflect compliments. When someone compliments our clothes, we shrug it off, "Oh, this old thing." The truth is, we don't need to say anything but, "Thank you."

When complimenting others, be sure it is not just idle flattery. Don't walk up to a group of friends and give each one a compliment. It doesn't look or feel sincere. Be specific. Rather than saying, "You look nice," why not be more explicit and proffer, "You look so skinny in those jeans!" or "I love your hair like that." When complimenting a significant other, do not rely solely on "you are so handsome/ beautiful." Compliment his/her eyes or smile and the quirks that make this person special. No one wants to be loved in generalities.

If you are complimented for a job well done, be gracious and acknowledge others who contributed. "I had a good team to work with" shows you appreciated their input. Don't take credit for things you didn't do. People resent glory hogs.

False humility is never becoming. If you are flattering people in hopes of some personal gain, your actions will be transparent.

People like to be around people who build and uplift others. They appreciate those who give sincere compliments, give credit where credit is due, and celebrate others' success.

Be that person.

The next time someone compliments me, I'm going to say:

_____

_____

Some things I like about my friends and family that I want them to know:

_____

_____

_____

_____

_____

CONVERSATION STARTERS

*W*e are often put in a position in which we don't know people. Sometimes we may be the odd man out and everyone else knows each other. Usually in this situation the others will make an attempt to get to know us and that relieves the pressure.

More often than not, we find ourselves in a room full of people who don't know each other. What do you say after "Hello"? At weddings and similar events you start out by asking how you know the couple. Share an amusing story you know about the bride or groom or their parents. At work related parties you ask what department the person works in and ask what they do.

At charity functions you ask how long they have lived in the area, where they came from, if they are affiliated with the charity sponsoring the event, if they have children, where their children go to school. Basically you are looking for common ground.

You can always ask what kind of work they do or what hobbies they enjoy.

Don't talk about the weather unless it has been particularly out of character for the season. The most important thing is to listen. Try to keep the other person talking as much as you can. Don't interrupt. Don't ask inappropriately personal questions (like how much money they make or how much they paid for their house.) Don't have a hidden agenda. Don't evaluate every person you met based upon what they can do for you.

What are some conversation starters that I could use?

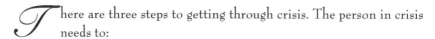

WHAT TO DO WHEN YOUR LOVED ONE IS IN CRISIS

*T*here are three steps to getting through crisis. The person in crisis needs to:

1. Talk about what happened.

2. Talk about how he or she feels about what happened.

3. Talk about what he or she plans to do about what happened.

Notice I said: talk, talk, talk. This should remind you that your role as a friend is to listen, listen, listen. God gave you two ears and one mouth. You need to use them proportionately.

The more you know about what your friend is going through, the better you will be equipped to help. Do a little research on the web.

Don't just be there during the crisis. Be there for the long haul (that's the hard part).

What would I want someone to do for me if I were in crisis?

_____

_____

NOTES:

_____

_____

WHAT TO DO WHEN YOUR LOVED ONE HAS A DEATH IN THE FAMILY

The first thing most people do when they hear the bad news is pick up the phone and call. Don't. Most people know at least five hundred people. Do you really think your friend would want the phone ringing five hundred times? Unless you are an immediate family member, a very close friend, or a neighbor, don't call until well after the funeral.

Don't worry about what to say. The most important thing you can do is "listen." It's okay to talk about the deceased. They need to talk. But don't ask for details. If they want to discuss them with you, they will.

There will be lots of attention up to and shortly after the funeral. The loneliness settles in later when people stop calling and visiting.

One of the best things you can do is to call on important dates, such as one month after death, two months, six months, and one year. These are days that your loved one will be feeling especially low. A phone call can be just the thing to lift one's spirit.

"I was just thinking about you and thought you might need a little company today. Would you like to go out for breakfast or lunch?" Or invite her to join you on a walk. Or you can stop by with a homemade goodie.

What You Can Say

Say, "I'm so sorry you have to go through this. How are you holding up? Would you like me to come over and help you?" Talk about the deceased and what a loss you feel. If you go through a receiving line at the funeral, say something like, "We are going to miss him/her," "I'll be over to see you in a few days," or "It was a lovely service." Don't feel like you have to say anything. A hug is really all the person needs. If it has been a long time since you have seen the family you might say, "I'm sorry we didn't have a chance to see you under better circumstances. If you need to get away for a few days, you know where we are. We'd love to have you come and stay with us."

If the person died after a long illness, you could say, "I've seen how hard this has been on you. Even though we all expected it, it's still hard to accept when it happens. How are you doing? Is there anything I can do for you?"

It's hard to know what to say about family members of our friends who have died that we never met. You could say something like, "I'm so sorry to hear about your mother's death. I never knew her, but I heard you talk about her and I know you had a very special relationship. I'm sure you'll miss her."

What You Can Do

Unless you are a family member or very close friend, don't call. Call someone who is a lot closer than you are and ask that person to offer your condolences and call you with the particulars about the funeral arrangements. Then you can pass the information on to others who may not be as close as you are. If you are a family member or very close friend, you might go over to the house and volunteer to answer the phone, take messages, and pass on information. This will leave the person free to make the funeral arrangements without the distraction of the phone and allow the person to return calls at his or her convenience.

Sending a card is one of the best things you can do. Make it personal. Handwrite (a typed note is impersonal) a short note about a special memory you have of the departed. Your friend will treasure those cards and read them over and over again through the years.

Death of a Child

The death of a child may be the hardest kind of tragedy to accept. A parent never expects to bury a child. It's unnatural. It's unfair. It's impossible to console a grieving mother or father. They don't want to hear, "It will be okay." It will *never* be okay.

They don't want to hear, "I know how you must feel." You can't possibly know unless you have actually lost a child yourself. It is better to say, "I can't even imagine how you must be feeling."

Don't say, "He's in a better place." How could there be a better place for a child to be than with their mother?

When you attend the funeral (and yes, you *must* attend) you don't need to worry about what to say. All you need to do is walk up to your friend and wrap your arms around her or him. "We're all here for you." There isn't time for everyone to have a conversation. There will be time for that later. Keep in touch.

What would I want someone to do for me if I were in this situation?

_____

_____

NOTES:

_____

_____

Death of a Teen

Losing a teenage son or daughter is devastating. The parents have come to learn the child's talents, hopes, and dreams. Those dreams have become their dreams as well. Just when the child seemed to have it all, the door was slammed in their face. The parents mourn the loss of the future that will never be, the family that will never be, the grandchildren they had assumed would come. They feel that it was not only their teen who was cheated, but they were also robbed of that future as well.

According to one statistical report, 5,000 youth aged 16–20 are killed in auto accidents every year. Of those, 75 percent of them aren't wearing seat belts. Instruct your teen to buckle up. For every teen killed, there are one or more survivors. These surviving teens need counseling to help them through their grieving process. A teen who was driving the car in a fatal accident carries a tremendous load of guilt, especially if there is reckless driving, alcohol, or drugs involved. They need professional help.

Parents of victims often want "justice" for their loss and want the state to prosecute the driver for negligence. I urge you to reconsider. Carrying the guilt for the rest of one's life will be more "justice" than any penalties that could be levied. Have mercy. What if it were your teen who was driving?

NOTES:

_____

_____

Death of a Spouse

Death is difficult no matter what the circumstances. An elderly woman does not want to hear that it is natural for the husband to go before the wife and that she should have expected it. She doesn't want to hear that he's in a better place. The best place is with her. Even after a long illness she might admit that he is finally free from pain and suffering. But as long as he was alive, there was hope. Now that hope is gone.

When death comes unexpectedly there is always sorrow over things that didn't get said or guilt over things that were said. Suggest that your friend write down all her feelings and read it, alone, at his gravesite. (This works for children too, but the gravesite is too traumatic. It is better for them to put their letters in helium balloons and watch them float up to "heaven" for their father to read.)

"I'm so sorry for your loss" is the generic line and is perfectly acceptable. Express your love and admiration for the departed. "I'll never forget the time . . ." "He had such a great personality, we'll all miss him so much." Offer to help: "I'm here for you any time, night or day, call me." That is comforting, but don't expect a call. It is up to you to keep in touch and anticipate her needs.

Don't rush the grieving period. It will take as long as it takes. Be sure to include this now single person in your social life.

What would I want someone to do for me if I were in this situation?

_____

_____

NOTES:

_____

_____

Miscarriage

*T*his is one of the most underestimated events in a woman's life. People seem to feel that since the baby was never born, the woman hasn't gotten attached to it. There are no shared experiences, etc. What's the big deal?

Believe me, it's a big deal to the woman. It is the death of a dream of a child that was to be hers and she will mourn that death.

I visited a friend in the hospital after she lost what would have been her third child. She was in tears when she told me I was the only one who had come to visit her. Don't minimize the loss by saying things like, "It wasn't meant to be," "It's God's will," or, "You'll get over it." It is better to say, "I'm so sorry for your loss, you must be so disappointed. Tell me how you are feeling." If the mother is worried about being able to become pregnant again, reassure her that she will.

Let her know it's okay to mourn. Realize that it can take as long as a year for her to recover emotionally, and whenever anyone asks her how many children she has, she will always mention the one she lost.

Visit her in the hospital. Visit her at home.

What would I want someone to do for me if I were in this situation?

_____

_____

NOTES:

_____

_____

Suicide

There was a student at my daughter's high school that committed suicide. He was a popular, smart, good looking, and wealthy kid that had everything going for him. His death sent a shockwave through the community because if he could do it, any one of our kids could be at risk. The school offered a class for kids who had thoughts of suicide. Two hundred kids signed up! (Total enrollment at that school was 2,000 kids, so that's 10%).

When someone commits suicide, the family is not only devastated by the death, but they have a whole additional spectrum of emotions to deal with: "How could I have prevented this?" "It's my fault for not seeing this coming."

"I should have done this, or I should have done that." "How could he have done this to me?"

Parents are racked with guilt. When they tell you it's all their fault, what can you say? You can look them square in the eye and say, "I just don't believe that. Parents make mistakes with their kids all the time and a lot worse mistakes than you ever made. Their kids don't kill themselves over it. I agree with you that it is terrible. I can't even imagine what you are going through right now. But don't blame yourself. Something just snapped in the kid. If he had been rational he wouldn't have done it. It is not your fault." Urge them to go to a support group. They need to hear how other parents have dealt with it. Continue to listen. Talking it out is part of recovery.

The parents of a teenager who has committed suicide will often find relief in helping prevent others from experiencing their pain. The parents can join a local support group, become proactive, and speak at local high schools, etc.

Allow the family time to grieve, but don't avoid them. Invite them to participate in activities and let them decide whether or not they are able to attend.

What You Can Do

An encounter with a suicidal person is always a deep emotional experience. There is the fear of not knowing what to do or doing the wrong thing. Just showing that you care is the most important thing you can do.

Develop a relationship of trust. Reassure the person. Listen and allow him to tell his story without interruption. Don't challenge or criticize him. Help calm his emotions. Be hopeful and help him gain self-control. Don't leave him alone. Stay with him or have someone stay with him. Urge him to seek counseling.

When you talk, be specific. Help the person sort out and categorize problems rather than deal with a huge, looming, unworkable problem. Help him recognize the central problem as compared to secondary problems.

Discuss alternative actions to help solve his problems.

There is always a part of a person that wants to live. Find it and build on it. It may be children, a spouse, ambitions, etc.

When someone talks of suicide, this is one time when you must not keep silent. When someone confides to you that he has nothing to live for or that he wishes he were dead, tell his spouse, if it is your friend. If it is a teenager, tell his parents. Report it to your clergy. Give the person one of the suicide hotline phone numbers at the end of this chapter and encourage him to call.

Warning Signs

Frequently there are warning signs. Suicide is often a carefully considered act, preceded by cries for help. Treat every threat as serious, but also as a cry to be saved.

If one is breaking off relationships, dropping out of activities, or suddenly giving away possessions, take action.

Sudden resolution of depression, with no apparent reason is also a symptom. (Often the suicide decision brings relief to the person due to finding a "way out" of his troubles.)

If your child obtains a weapon, this is a big-time warning sign that trouble is ahead. (Sixty-five percent of suicides of those under the age of 25 were committed with guns. In the 15–19 age group it was 81 percent.)

More than one third of all suicides are drug-related.

Myths and Facts

Myth: The tendency toward suicide is inherited.

Fact: Suicide has no characteristic or genetic quality.

Myth: Suicidal persons are mentally ill.

Fact: Many persons who have attempted or completed suicide would not have been diagnosed as mentally ill.

Myth: Asking a person if he or she is suicidal will lead them into an attempt.

Fact: Asking a direct, caring question will often minimize and diffuse the anxiety and can act as a suicide deterrent.

Myth: Good circumstances prevent suicide.

Fact: Frequently the opposite is true. Persons of means and education are sometimes more highly at risk of destructive behavior.

Myth: Motive for or causes of suicide are established and determined.

Fact: Suicide is a lengthy and complex pattern of behavior where precise
motives are difficult to ascertain. Each case of suicide can be as complex as the person who completed it.

There used to be a stigma attached to suicide. People wouldn't talk about
it. Today, however, with people such as Katherine Hepburn, Mikhail
Baryshnikov, Peter Fonda and Joan Rivers openly speaking about the suicides in their families, it has opened the door for others.

Do a search on the Internet for suicide prevention sites.

What would I do if someone told me they were thinking about suicide?

_____

_____

NOTES:

_____

_____

HOW TO EXPLAIN DEATH TO CHILDREN

The best way to help children cope with their loss is to answer their
questions and let them talk about the loss. Don't force them to open
up. Ask children to tell you about fun things they remember doing with the
deceased. Don't trivialize their feelings. Expect behavior changes. Don't

explain death as a trip or as sleep. Children may fear future vacations or bedtime as a result.

If you believe in God and heaven, tell the child that the person went to heaven to live with God. And once you go there, you can't come back. The person didn't want us to be sad, he's in a better place than earth and he has important things to do there. God needed him now and couldn't wait for a time that was "convenient" for all of us. We will see him again when it is our turn to go to heaven and he'll be very happy to see us again.

We can still talk to the person through our prayers. We can ask God to take good care of him and give him messages from us. The person will always live on in our memories.

Have the child write a letter to the deceased person, saying goodbye and how much they miss them, then put the letter in a balloon and let it fly up into the air.

If you don't believe in a hereafter, you can still reassure the child that the person is in peace and that they will no longer feel any hurt or pain. He just stopped living—just as when a toy stops working when the batteries go dead. But there are no batteries for people. We can break lots of things in our bodies and be fixed, but when the part of us that makes us live gets broken, we can't be fixed.

NOTES:

_____

_____

WHAT TO DO WHEN YOUR LOVED ONE IS DEALING WITH DEPRESSION

*D*epression is a real disease. Contrary to popular belief, it is not unhappiness, sadness, or grief over adversity, although these things can trigger depression.

Depression is on the rise. There are ten times as many people diagnosed with depression as there used to be and the average age of the first diagnosis has dropped from twenty-eight to fourteen. What's happening? Some think parents have taken self-esteem too far. In the process of developing self-esteem, many have spent so much time trying to make their children feel good about themselves and have done so much for them that they have not adequately prepared their children to deal with failure.

In this day and age, there is no reason for someone to suffer. If your friend has feelings of depression, she should see her doctor.

I'd do the following for someone who is either "clinically" depressed or simply feeling depressed.

- invite to a movie

- take out to breakfast or lunch

- go for a walk together

- exercise together

- invite to a picnic at a park, lake, or beach

- offer to clean house or do laundry

- give a female friend a jar of bath salts or bubble bath to enjoy in the tub
- give her a gift certificate for a day of beauty at a local spa or salon
- invite a male friend to join you in a round of golf or invite him to a sporting event
- give him a gym membership for a month

What would I want someone to do for me if I were in this situation?

_____

_____

NOTES:

_____

_____

HOW CAN I HELP WHEN A DISASTER STRIKES?

*W*hen disasters hit (earthquakes, fires, floods, hurricanes, tornadoes, etc.), help is needed immediately. If you live by an area just hit, what can you do?

Load up your car with emergency supplies and get as close as you can to help. Listen to the news to find out where relief stations are being set up. Don't call the Red Cross unless it's an emergency because their lines will be flooded with calls from people who need help.

Don't go near the area unless you really plan to work. If you are just delivering supplies, get in and out as quickly as possible. "Looky-loos" just get in the way and impede the efforts of the rescue workers. Don't bring a camera. Extra bodies moving around and flashing lights are distracting and slow down the rescue efforts.

Volunteers are often needed to help "dig out" survivors. Bring heavy gloves, a shovel, and a hard hat if you have one. (Rags, old shoes, work clothes, etc., are needed for cleanup and salvage work.)

Urgent Needs

- water
- paper cups
- diapers
- baby formula
- milk
- shoes
- blankets
- extra clothing
- sanitary napkins
- medical supplies (bandages, gauze, antiseptic)
- flashlights

Short-Term Needs

- food
- hygiene supplies (razors, soap, shampoo, toilet paper, Kleenex, etc.)
- paper plates, utensils
- games for children to play, cards, books

• pet food

What kind of emergency is most likely to happen in my area?

_____

_____

What I would be willing to do in an emergency?

_____

_____

WHAT TO DO WHEN YOUR LOVED ONE HAS BEEN DIAGNOSED WITH A DISEASE THAT YOU'RE NOT FAMILIAR WITH

1. Find out all you can about the disease or condition. Go to the library. Search the web. (Try helpingothers.ws and click on "Diseases and Conditions.")

2. Be optimistic. Site examples of people who have lived successfully with the disease or condition. Don't dwell on those who have died.

3. Remind your friend that medical advances are being made on a daily basis and there could be a cure just around the corner.

4. Greet your friend by saying, "You are really doing great" or "You look really good (if he or she does look good—if not, don't say it)." Your

friend needs all the encouragement you can give. But compliments must be sincere, not patronizing.

5. Offer to drive your friend to treatments. Go out to lunch afterward.

6. Bring dinner over to the family. Be sure to ask if there are any dietary restrictions.

7. Be aware of your friend's moods. If tired or grumpy, he or she may not be getting enough sleep. Volunteer to take over some morning or afternoon tasks so he or she can take a nap.

8. Put yourself in your friend's shoes. What do you think you would like someone to do for you?

9. If it is your friend's child who is diagnosed with the disease or condition, treat the child as you normally do. Say how sorry you are for this inconvenience in his or her life. A little gift would be appropriate if the child is in the hospital. Special attention is fine as long as it is not overdone to the point where siblings get neglected. If you visit, don't stay too long.

10. Support whatever decisions the patient has made about treatment. If the person is unsure about courses of treatments, suggest that the patient seek a second opinion.

11. Be a sounding board for your friend. Listen to the person's concerns and fears and be a source of comfort, reassurance, and support. Provide as much normalcy to the person's life as possible.

12. Be sensitive to the caregiver. Offer to stay with the patient for several hours so the caregiver can have some time off.

What would I want someone to do for me if I were in this situation?

_____

_____

NOTES:

_____

_____

HOW TO HELP A LOVED ONE WHO IS DEALING WITH DIVORCE

*J*f your friend is the party being left behind by a husband who has found "another woman," it is going to be more painful than if she initiated the split. Your friend is going to experience a loss equal to that of death and she will mourn that relationship. Your friend needs to realize that every marriage ends either by death or divorce, and that she is not alone. (The National Center for Health statistics reports that there are 2.4 million marriages every year and 1.2 million divorces every year.) The grieving process takes time. She should expect to mourn 1 year for every 5 years she was married. Encourage her to be patient.

The most important thing you can do for your friend is to be there for her. Don't avoid her because you don't know what to say. Let her talk. She is tired of bottling up her feelings. She needs to vent her emotions. Don't tell her she shouldn't be feeling this way or that. She feels what she feels. She'll get over it in time and return to the person you once knew.

Don't say "I know how you feel" (unless you have been through it yourself). Instead say, "You must be feeling awful. I can't even imagine what you are going through."

You can say "Don't be so hard on yourself" or "Why are you blaming yourself? It takes two to make a marriage work. He wasn't willing to do his part." "He betrayed your trust."

If, on the other hand, she is blaming him for everything, let her. Don't chime in with things she might have done to prevent it. It's too late.

What would I want someone to do for me if I were in this situation?

NOTES:

HOW TO TELL THE CHILDREN YOU'RE GETTING A DIVORCE

Divorce is a very traumatic experience for children, regardless of their age. The world, as they know it, comes crashing down around them and they don't know what to expect for their future. What will happen to them? Who will take care of them?

Some parents are so worried about their children's reaction that they don't tell them for months. They just keep saying, "Daddy's on a trip." They are just postponing the inevitable. The children need to be told. It's far better to be told by their own parents than by their friends who hear about it from their parents. If you don't tell the child and he learns from another source, he is not only losing the home and family he once knew, but he is also losing feelings of security and trust.

Be honest . . . sort of. Don't go into detail about your marital troubles. Don't blame your spouse. Don't force your child to take sides. Reassure the children that they had nothing to do with your decision. It was just a problem between you and your spouse that couldn't be resolved. Tell the children that you both love them and want to be with them as much as possible (that's why you have to go to court to let a judge decide how much time you each get to spend with them).

Don't make promises you can't keep.

NOTES:

_____

_____

WHAT TO DO WHEN YOUR CHILD CATCHES YOU DOING SOMETHING WRONG

*Y*ou start cussing at someone who just cut you off and your children are in the car, you are caught in a lie, your child sees you drunk, you get in a fight at a soccer game, etc. Don't try to justify your actions. Say,

"I'm sorry. I shouldn't have said/done that." Use the incident as a teaching moment and explain to your child the proper way to handle similar situations. Explain that we all lose control at times but that it isn't right to do so. Apologize to your child. Where possible, apologize to the other people involved. Display genuine remorse.

Your children will learn how to apologize from you.

What would I do?

_____

_____

What do I do or say in front of my children that is sending the wrong message?

_____

_____

WHAT TO SAY WHEN YOU DON'T KNOW WHAT TO SAY

*D*on't avoid your friend because you don't know what to say. The bottom line is, it is not what you say that is important. It is the fact that you care. Just call and say, "I was just thinking about you. How are you doing?" Don't be afraid to say, "I have no idea what to say, I just wanted to be here for you."

Don't underestimate the healing power of a warm smile and a big hug.

There is a song that I really like called *When You Say Nothing At All* by Ronan Keating that says it best:

"It's amazing how you can speak right to my heart
Without saying a word you can light up the dark . . .
The smile on your face let's me know that you need me
There's a truth in your eyes saying you'll never leave me
The touch of your hand says you'll catch me whenever I fall
You say it best when you say nothing at all."

Sometimes, for fear of saying the wrong thing we do nothing at all. Later, when we see our friend around town, our guilt at our neglect sometimes causes us to further avoid any contact. If time has passed, it is never too late to do the right thing. If you failed to be there for a friend in a time of need, apologize. Explain the feelings of fear or inadequacy that kept you away. Do not justify your absence. Ask forgiveness. Depending upon the circumstances and the amount of time that has passed, your friend might not welcome you back into his/her life. Nonetheless, you can be at peace with yourself for attempting to make restitution.

What would I be comfortable saying?

HOW TO TALK INTOXICATED FRIENDS OUT OF THEIR KEYS AFTER A PARTY AT YOUR HOUSE

*Y*ou need to be aware of the fact that if it's your party; you can and will be held responsible in a court of law if any partygoer is involved in a drunk driving accident.

How can you protect yourself?

You have to make every effort to be sure that your guests do not drink and drive. Plan to stop serving alcohol at a certain time and offer coffee and food for the last hour. (Be aware, however, that some guests will leave once the bar is closed. Unless you can control the hour *all* of your guests depart, you will need to take other precautions as well.)

Collect your guest's keys at the onset of the party so that they must come to you when they are departing. If you are timid and don't want to tell your guests when they've had too much to drink (or if you want to be able to enjoy the party without having to screen each and every one of your friends upon departure), hire someone to do it for you.

Hire a bartender to decide who's had too much to drink and stop serving him. If you let your guests pour their own drinks, it is very difficult to monitor potential problems.

Hire a bouncer to collect the keys of those who have been drinking and to place people in cabs. (Bouncers are also handy if any aggression ensues.)

You might also consider hiring transportation to drive people home who have had too much to drink. Or call for cabs. There are also organizations in many cities that provide this service for free.

You may think you can't afford these extra precautions, but they are nothing compared to what it would cost you if someone got in an accident on the way home from your party and you were sued for damages.

NOTES:

_____

_____

HOW TO HANDLE A POTENTIALLY EMBARRASSING SITUATION

*W*hat if you notice someone's fly is unzipped, they have something in their teeth, or there is toilet paper stuck to the bottom of their shoe? Always tell the person, but in a delicate manner. Don't tell anyone else and don't call anyone else's attention to it. Tell the person as discretely as possible and down play the situation.

You don't have to be a close friend or family member. People may feel embarrassed, but they will be more so the longer it goes unchecked. If they have something between their teeth, just say "you have a little something right there" and point to your own teeth where it is.

NOTES:

_____

_____

WHAT TO SAY WHEN YOUR THIRTY-YEAR OLD FRIEND GETS ENGAGED

*S*ay the same things you would say if she were in her early twenties. Saying, "Congratulations" to a woman has never been acceptable (it makes it sound like you are surprised that she was able to snag a man. "Congratulations" is what you say to the young man, presumably because he is so lucky to get such a good woman). Saying congratulations to a thirty plus woman is really rude. It ranks right up there with, "Finally, we were beginning to think you were never going to get married." The worst I've ever heard personally was, "See, I told you if you lowered your standards you'd be able to find someone." Ouch.

Why not say, "I'm so excited for you. Let's see the ring. Have you set the date yet? How did he propose? Details, girl, details." If you haven't seen her in a long time and don't know her fiancé, ask, "What's he like? Where did you meet him?" etc.

What would I say?

_____

_____

WHAT TO SAY WHEN YOUR LOVED ONE GETS A FACE-LIFT

*T*here will come a day when your over fifty friend will show up with a new face. If you see her within three months of the procedure, you may be faced with a dilemma: Do you lie and tell her she looks great, or do you tell the truth and tell her she made a huge mistake?

Lie, and I'll tell you why. It takes several months for everything to settle in. In the weeks following surgery, the skin will appear too tight, her eyes will either look like a gremlin, wookiee, or like they are unnaturally slanted. So, after your initial gasp for breath say, "I know what you've been up to . . . you are going to look fantastic." Don't ask for details unless she offers them. And, *never* ask how much it cost!

Six months later you'll think she looks great. After one year, don't be surprised to find yourself seriously considering it.

Always tell the person they didn't need to do it, but they sure look great. Insurance doesn't cover cosmetic surgery so it cost her plenty. Be generous with your compliments. "You look ten years younger" is what she's hoping to hear. Indulge her.

MY COMMENTS:

_____

_____

HOW DO YOU DEAL WITH FRIENDS OR FAMILY WHOSE FINANCIAL SITUATION IS FAR ABOVE OR BELOW YOURS?

One thing that never changes in life is that things change. Two sisters will marry and one's husband will suddenly find himself on a fast track to the top of his company. While the other sister's husband works like a dog to get ahead but never seems to get a break. It wouldn't be unusual for there to be some resentment and/or jealousy by the one who feels like the "ugly stepsister" whose sister married the handsome prince and rode off into the sunset to live happily ever after

Is the rich sister supposed to share her husband's earnings with her sister to keep things even? Of course not.

We all have to learn to live within our means. If we have more than those we love, we need to be sensitive to their financial restraints and not ask them to participate in things they can't afford. Invite them over for a backyard bar-becue, an evening of board games, to watch movies, or for other family oriented activities.

If you have a vacation home, you can invite them to use it (with or without you). You can treat them to a nice dinner, theatre, or ball game once in a while. But if you always take them to the best restaurants, the most expensive theatre seats, or the owner's box at the Padres games, they may think you are rubbing their noses in your newfound wealth.

Don't be afraid to be generous, but be aware that sometimes excessive generosity can be misconstrued. There's a fine line between sharing and showing off.

Your wealthy relative or friend may appear to have it all, but wealth has a completely different set of challenges. Just because you don't see or hear about them, doesn't mean they don't exist. Elvis, Marilyn Monroe, Janis Joplin, and Jim Belushi had what seemed to be everything you could ever hope for: money, fame, and status. But they were so miserable they turned to drugs to fill the emptiness inside.

The secret to a happy life is to make the most of what you have and count your blessings. If you are always looking at what you lack or comparing yourself to others, you will never be happy.

Am I better off, or worse off than my peers? _____

Has it been a problem in the past? _____

Could it be in the future? _____

How would I handle it? _____

_____

WHAT TO SAY WHEN YOUR FRIEND BUYS ALL NEW FURNITURE—AND YOU HATE IT

She's not asking you whether she should buy it or not. She bought it. You know she loves it. You'd better find something you like about it. "Wow, what a difference."

"I never would have thought to put those colors together." "You are so creative."

If the sofa is comfortable to sit in, say so, "It's so comfortable." Look around, maybe there is an accent piece you love. "I love the lamps."

She's excited, so you be excited for her. We all have different tastes. Just be glad you don't have to live with it. (Chances are she's not crazy about your furniture.)

MY COMMENTS:

_____

_____

WHAT TO SAY WHEN YOUR LOVED ONES BECOME GRANDPARENTS

When I got married my mother urged me not to get pregnant right away, "Not," she said, "because I'm not ready to be a grandmother, but I just can't stand the thought of sleeping with a grandfather."

Now it's my turn. I've been waiting a long time to be a grandma. When you hit sixty it seems like the major topic of discussion among your friends is their grandchildren. I've been feeling a little left out. However, my day has finally arrived. My oldest daughter, Amy, gave birth to an adorable boy, Lincoln Paul Jones on June 14th (Flag Day) 2006. He is the light of my life—and well worth the wait.

I know I'll never keep up with my friends who have over twenty grandchildren and are now counting great grandchildren.

Just keep in mind that for every young woman having a baby, there are grandparents standing by. I appreciated the fact that at my daughter's baby shower someone actually gave me a gift (a small photo album for my purse called a Brag Book to show off baby photos.)

Just having people say, "Hi, how are you enjoying being a grandma?" makes me feel great . . . and loved. (And it gives me an excuse to whip out my Brag Book.)

MY COMMENTS:

_____

_____

HOW TO RECOGNIZE A HEART ATTACK OR STROKE

These are the most common symptoms of a heart attack:

1. Chest pain. Most heart attacks involve discomfort in the center of the chest that lasts for more than a few minutes or goes away and comes

back. The discomfort can feel like uncomfortable pressure, squeezing, fullness, or pain. Some people have mistaken it for indigestion.

2. Pain in other areas of the upper body. Can include pain or discomfort in one or both arms, neck, jaw, stomach, or back. (It can be as high as your shoulder, upper back, particularly the left side, and under your arm.)

3. Shortness of breath. Often comes along with chest pain. But it also can occur before other symptoms.

4. Other symptoms. May include breaking out in a cold sweat, nausea, or light-headedness. Women have come to the emergency room with severe hip pain caused by a heart attack.

5. Difficulty breathing while lying down. If you have to sit up to breathe you could be having congestive heart failure.

If you experience *any* pain that won't go away and is severe enough to make you feel nauseated, have someone drive you to the hospital, or call 911.

If you are alone and experiencing these symptoms, call 911. Take an aspirin. If you feel faint, you may only have ten seconds before passing out. Take a deep breath and cough as hard as you can. Repeat the deep breath and cough every two seconds until the ambulance gets there. (The deep breath gets oxygen into the lungs and the cough keeps the blood circulating).

If you are with someone who is not breathing, call 911 then begin CPR. (If you don't know CPR, take a class. Everyone should know how to do it).

If you feel tired all the time, get winded after very little exertion, and/or your legs feel weak and tired, it is not "just getting old." It may be *clogged arteries!* See your doctor.

You can tell if a person is having a stroke by asking the victim three simple questions:

1. Ask the individual to smile.

2. Ask him or her to raise both arms.

3. Ask the person to speak a simple sentence coherently (e.g. "It is sunny out today.")

If he or she has trouble with *any* of these tasks, call 911 immediately and describe the symptoms to the dispatcher.

WHAT TO DO WHEN YOUR CHILDREN SUFFER HEARTBREAKS

*P*ain is a lamentable but inevitable part of growing up. Yet parents have a difficult time knowing how to handle their children's problems. When your toddler falls and scrapes her knee, when your little boy is cut from the football team, when your teenage daughter is dumped by the boy of her dreams . . . it's difficult to know what to say and/or do.

Always take your child's problem seriously. It may appear trivial to you, but in your child's mind it might mean the world. A small scratch may appear painless or a break-up might actually be a relief to you, but your child is hurting and needs to feel your love and concern.

Do not attempt to solve your child's problem for them. Most children do not come to their parents looking for a solution, rather they are looking for a sign of care, concern, and compassion. Reassure your child that your love is unconditional. Your love is not contingent upon your child's grades, athletic abilities, or social status.

No matter how much you would love to resolve the issue, your daughter's boyfriend will probably not take her back, the football coach will not reconsider, and you can't take the scrape away. What your teen is seeking is the same as what your toddler is seeking: the proverbial kiss to make it better. Does kissing a boo-boo actually heal the pain? Of course not. But what the child is actually seeking is a demonstration of love and concern, sympathy with the pain he/she is feeling.

Tell your son how special he is. "You would have added something very special to the team. It's too bad they couldn't see that."

Tell your daughter that she deserves to be treated better. "I know you must be feeling terrible right now. I wish I had a magic wand to make you feel better. It's going to take some time, but the pain really will go away. Let's you and I make some plans to keep busy for a while to take your mind off things. I know there's someone out there who is just perfect for you and who will see all that I see in you."

Try to remember back when something similar happened to you. What would have helped you?

How do I/would I handle my children's heartaches?

_____

_____

WHAT TO DO WHEN YOU ENCOUNTER HOMELESS PEOPLE BEGGING ON THE STREET CORNER

*W*e've all heard the stories of the "homeless" person on the street corner who, at the end of the day walks around the block to his Cadillac. I had a personal experience with a guy whose sign read "Will work for food." I had a car full of groceries so I pulled over and told him to help himself. He could have all of it and I'd go get more.

His response was, "I don't want your food lady. I need cash." But you can't let a few bad apples stop you from helping those truly in need. Approximately 1% of the U.S. population experience homelessness each year, 38% of them being children (Urban Institute 2000). That translates to 3.5 million!

If you want to give and are financially able to do so, good for you. It is never "wrong" to want to help your fellow man. To those who argue that the person may not in fact be needy or may be using the funds to support an addiction, you can always argue that the way they use the funds is between them and their God, but you won't allow their choices to keep you from doing the right thing.

For those who want to give but have limited resources, you may want to donate where you can do the most good (e.g., a local homeless shelter or soup kitchen). You might also consider buying gift certificates from McDonald's or Denny's and handing those out. At least you'll know they will be able to get a meal (and not be able to trade it in for drugs or alcohol). You could also have some cards made up with the address of your town's homeless shelter and pass those out.

Where is the homeless shelter in my town?

_____

NOTES:

_____

_____

WHAT TO SAY WHEN YOU FIND OUT YOUR FRIEND'S CHILD IS HOMOSEXUAL

*O*uch. I was hoping to avoid this one. But there is so much going on in that community that we can't just look the other way anymore. Times have changed and we have to learn to deal with it. Typically, in our society, when a homosexual person comes out of the closet, the parents are likely to go into the closet. They are living in the past. They wonder what they did to "cause" it. They think others won't look at them the same anymore. They live in denial and secrecy. Keep this in mind when you want to talk to your friend.

First, how did you "find out?" Did the mother of the child tell you or did you find out through the "grapevine?"

If you found out through the grapevine, and it is not generally known, I'd not bring it up for two reasons. One, your friend may think no one knows, and if you bring it up, your friend will wonder who else knows and be very anxious about it. And, two, there is a possibility that your friend may not know, and it is not your place to tell her.

I'd bring up the subject in a very innocent and nonthreatening way. Such as, "Oprah (or whoever) had an interesting show on homosexuals the other day. It wasn't the typical shock value show, it was very real and got me thinking about how I'd handle it if I found out my child was gay." Test the waters, show that you would not be judgmental and maybe your friend will open up to you. If not, drop it. If she does bring it up, offer to help any way you can.

If your friend does confide in you, that is not an indication that it's okay to spread the word. This is one of those areas where your friend will be very selective in whom she confides. Keep the confidence. Your friend needs someone. Be there and show your support. Don't avoid bringing up the child's name. Treat the child like all your friend's other children. Don't bring up your moral convictions unless you are asked. It is not your place to moralize.

What would I want someone to do for me if I were in this situation?

_____

NOTES:

_____

_____

IS HONESTY ALWAYS THE BEST POLICY?

*W*e hear these mantras over and over again. "Honesty is the best policy," "Always tell the truth," "Be honest with me," etc. But is honesty the best policy in every situation? I don't think so. We should be honest, but not *brutally* honest. Here are my guidelines:

If you tell your friend the truth, is there anything she can do about it?

Is telling the truth going to make her life better or be hurtful?

Would you want someone to tell you this?

There are a few specific situations in this book to give you examples. Review "What to Say When Your Loved One Gets a Face-Lift," and "What to Say When Your Friend Buys All New Furniture—and You Hate It."

Sometimes we owe it to the other person to be honest. If you are going to be married, your partner should know as much about you as possible. It is dishonest to withhold the truth about yourself (including *relevant* information about your past) from someone you are thinking of joining your life with. It is a lie of omission.

It's similar to trying to sell a house that has cracks in the foundation, but because they happened 10 years ago and were fixed, there would be no need to mention it. That's illegal in the real estate world. All damage and repairs, no matter when they happened, are by law to be disclosed so that the buyer is fully informed.

That doesn't mean you have to go into all the gory details. While honesty is imperative in a marriage, the details are not. If your spouse asks you a question like how many people you've slept with, it's best to side step it. Unless you can tell him "you're the only one," don't give him a number. You can never take it back. Once he knows the number, it is something that could wound his pride, lower his opinion of you, and eat away at him.

Before marriage, be vague and talk in generalities, but if they press the issue, they want to know and you have an obligation to tell them. Have you ever cheated on your past loves? Have you ever had any addictions? Make sure to address these issues.

After marriage, there is nothing they can do about it. It could harm your relationship to start fessing up. However, if you had any addictions that didn't get disclosed before marriage, your partner should be aware of them so in times of stress he could watch for signs that might send you back.

What it really comes down to are those three questions above.

NOTES:

_____

_____

HOW TO HELP A FRIEND OR FAMILY MEMBER WHO IS IN THE HOSPITAL

*W*hen a family member or friend is ill, it affects the well-being of the entire family. The more serious the condition the more stress will be placed on the family. Everyone wants to care for the patient, but it is important that those who are coming to the aid of the patient are taking good care of themselves as well. They need to eat regular meals, get sufficient sleep, and keep themselves in good spirits so they can support the patient's needs.

Keep in mind that visits and telephone calls interfere with the patient's opportunities to sleep and rest. As mentioned above, in serious situations, the family is under a great deal of stress and a flood of phone calls would be inappropriate. Rather than disturb the family, you can call the nurse's station in the intensive care unit and they can tell you if and when to visit.

It might be better to visit with the family members who are in the waiting room to get updates on the patient's condition (the nurse's station won't give you that information), instead of visiting the patient. Let the family relay your get-well wishes.

When visiting patients in the intensive care unit, you need to observe more stringent rules. Some rules include: no fresh flowers, only two visitors at a time, only immediate family members, and no one under 14.

When the patient is in standard recovery rooms the rules are more relaxed, but you should still exercise good judgment. Don't tire the patient by too many visitors and by staying too long. (Try to limit your visit to twenty minutes or less.)

Again, it is best to call before you visit to be sure it is okay to visit. Some people don't want any visitors. As I mentioned earlier, when my mother was in the hospital, she didn't want anyone to see her in the hospital—not even her grown children. Conversely, I have a friend who would never speak to me again if I didn't visit her in the hospital; and she expects flowers and balloons to boot. There is no "one-size-fits-all" approach to relationships. So, when in doubt, ask.

If the patient welcomes visits, it is best to check in with the nurse's station first to make sure you are coming at a convenient time. If too many people show up at once, don't hang out in the hall to chat. That disturbs other patients. Wait in the hospital's waiting room.

If you would like to bring something for the patient, you might consider chapstick, a warm blanket, a CD player with soothing music (Bach, Mozart, smooth jazz, meditation music), slippers, socks (to keep their feet warm), a bed jacket for women, a robe (for walking the halls), magazines, etc. Books are better choices for when they return home from the hospital because it is difficult to read when on most medications.

Check with the nursing staff before bringing in any food items. Most patients are on special diets.

Don't forget: It is not about you. It might make *you* feel better to hang out with your friend or family member, but you must respect the patient's wishes.

If you have to travel a long distance to visit a family member in the hospital, you might consider staying at a hotel rather than staying with the family. All their attention should be focused on the patient rather than trying to entertain and feed you and your family.

NOTES:

_____

_____

HOW TO GET ALONG WITH YOUR IN-LAWS

*I*deally, we love the people our children will decide to marry and we welcome them into our family and treat them like our own children. However, this is not a perfect world and sometimes we disapprove of our kid's choice in a mate. If this is the case, suck it up and pretend to accept it. You don't have to live with that person the rest of your life. Your son or daughter has different needs than you. If the person really is a scoundrel, he will be found out and your daughter will have to deal with him—not you. When that happens, be supportive—no "I told you so's." You don't want your child to stay with him just to spite you.

If you treat your child's spouse badly, he won't want to step foot in your house. That will certainly put a strain on your child's relationship with you. Is that what you want?

If this sounds like what has been going on in your family, apologize for your behavior and start treating the spouse as if he were your own child (but without the lectures).

When dealing with your in-laws, your first line of defense is your spouse. Your spouse should not allow his/her parents to be disrespectful and make it plain that if the behavior continues you will distance yourself from them. If your spouse can't stand up to his/her parents, you'll have to fight your own battle. The best way to do that is to try little acts of kindness. Be so charming that they can't possibly find anything to criticize. If they start criticizing you in the presence of your children say, "I'm sorry you feel that way about me. But I can't let you speak to me like this in front of our children and if you continue to do so we will have to leave."

Treat each other as if you already have the relationship you were wishing for and it will come.

How would I handle a conflict with my in-laws?

_____

_____

My father-in-law would love it if I _____

My mother-in-law would love it if I _____

WHAT DO YOU DO WHEN YOUR SPOUSE HAS AN INTEREST OR HOBBY YOU DON'T SHARE?

*I*s your husband a sports nut? Is he addicted to video games, power tools, fishing, hunting, poker, golf, etc.? Unless the pastime could prove harmful to himself or your family, be supportive. This doesn't mean you must embrace the hobby yourself, but you can find ways to support him from the sidelines. If it's football he loves, offer to host a Super Bowl party for him and his friends. Surprise him with tickets to a game. If he's a golfer, buy him a new club or suggest a family vacation near a great golf course. A little interest goes a long way toward making him feel you care about him and his passions.

If something is important to your spouse, you can support him without having to embrace it yourself. Let him do his thing without having to listen to you complain about it. The more you support his interests/hobbies, the more he'll support yours.

Caveat: There are times when your husband's interest has a destructive influence on your family. If his passion is pornography or gambling, if his involvement with sports becomes fanatical, or if any pastime becomes so consuming that he engages in it at all available times and at the expense of his children, it is time to draw the line. Explain that you are fully supportive of him pursuing positive venues, but that moderation is the key. Make a compromise that he can watch the football game while you take care of the kids, if he will watch them before or after so you get some alone time to take a bubble bath, read, or watch a television show of your choosing. And if his love of sports extends not just to football, basketball, and baseball seasons, but also golf, tennis, soccer, bowling, darts, and dodge ball events as well, make him prioritize. It is not reasonable to spend all day every day in front of ESPN.

What do I/would I do?

WHAT TO SAY TO A LOVED ONE WHO IS UNHAPPY ABOUT A JOB TRANSFER

*M*oving is always stressful, even when the family is looking forward to the change. Not only is it a huge amount of work, but there are nagging questions, like: Will we like the new area? Will we like the people there? Will they like us? With the proper attitude, the answer will most likely be yes.

Moving can be very traumatic if it is an unwelcome change. People can go through emotions that are very similar to the grief one experiences following the death of a loved one. This kind of stress can trigger depression.

It can be very difficult for you to have your best friend move not only out of the city, but out of the state.

Support her and the decision her family has made. Help her pack and label.

Bring lunch or dinner over. When you are packing, it's difficult to stop to prepare meals and the ingredients or utensils may already be packed away.

Gift idea: Use an empty box of detergent ("Fresh Start" would be particularly appropriate) and fill it with things your friend might like to take with her, such as a framed photo of you and your family or a gift certificate to a store like Crate and Barrel (be sure there is a store in the location where the family is moving).

After she has gone, call to see how she's getting along in the new place. Drop her a line or an email occasionally to let her know she is still in your thoughts. Try to visit her every couple of years or so and invite her to come visit you.

What would I want someone to do for me if I were moving?

_____

_____

NOTES:

_____

_____

HOW SHOULD YOU REACT TO SECOND, THIRD, OR FOURTH MARRIAGES?

It is not unusual anymore for someone to be married more than once. People do make mistakes so they may get divorced and remarry, or they marry again after the death of their spouse.

However, when someone gets divorced, remarries, and gets divorced again, it's easy to be skeptical of their next planned nuptials. How do you get excited and support them—and should you?

If she's excited, you should be excited. Who knows, the third (or fourth) time may be the one that will last forever. Your job is to assume it will. Go ahead and buy the couple a crystal vase engraved with their initials, or monogrammed pillowcases.

At the first sign of trouble you might suggest they see a marriage counselor. She may be surprised to learn that all the blame of her earlier failed marriages weren't solely the fault of her ex's. There may be some issues she needs to work on, but it's not your job to point that out.

What would I do if I had a friend who was marrying for the third or fourth time? Would I be able to support that marriage?

_____

_____

HOW TO DECIDE WHICH MILESTONE PARTY INVITATIONS TO ATTEND

*R*esponding to wedding invitations, bridal showers, baby showers, anniversaries, 50th birthday parties, and other celebrations has always been a dilemma to me. How do you know when to go and when to decline?

Major events are expensive and the cost of food is often per head, so I used to fear that I could create a financial burden by attending. However, after planning two weddings for my own daughters I've come to realize that when people invite you, they really want you to attend. If they have financial restraints, their invitation list has already taken that into account. If you are still on the invitation list, it is because they are hoping you will attend.

On occasion, an invitation list is extensive to avoid alienating anyone in the office, church, or other organization. My rule of thumb has boiled down to this: If I'm being invited along with everyone else in a group, I make up my mind according to how well I know the person. If I think they would have invited me even if they weren't inviting everyone, then I make an effort to go. If I don't really know the person that well, I don't go.

Bear in mind, when people are planning a large gathering, it is important to them that it *is* a large gathering. The more people who attend the more loved the individual feels.

If you are invited to a smaller gathering, the fact that your name appears on the limited guest list indicates that they truly want you to attend.

If you live out of state, they don't expect you to come, but if you did, they would be thrilled. People who make the effort to attend by traveling long distances send a message to the guest of honor that they are truly valued and loved. How great is that.

Remember: while you may receive dozens of wedding invitations each year, this is the only one honoring this particular couple. It is a momentous occasion for them and deserves to be treated as such.

In the future, consider an invitation to a milestone event to be a request for your *presence*—not your *present*.

MY COMMENTS:

_____

_____

_____

_____

HOW DO YOU FELLOWSHIP NEW MEMBERS AT CHURCH?

*I*f you see people you haven't met, walk up to them and say, "I haven't seen you here before. Are you visiting?" If they say yes, ask them where they are visiting from and what brought them to your area.

If you find out that the family has just moved in, guide them to where their classes are. Introduce them to others. Find out the ages of their children and introduce them to someone who has children their age or who lives in their area. Be sure they get invited to church socials or any other upcoming events. Be on the look out for them each week so that you can at least say hello (and try to call them by name).

If you ever see new people sitting alone, go sit by them.

OTHER IDEAS:

_____

_____

WHAT TO DO FOR NEW NEIGHBORS

*I*f new people are moving in, go over and offer assistance. Bring them lunch or dinner. Welcome them to the neighborhood. Give them your telephone number so they can call you if they need anything. If that's not your style, at least wave a warm welcome to acknowledge them.

Bring a basket of items you think might help the family settle into their new community, such as a map, the local newspaper or magazine, or a list of your favorite service providers (hairdresser, doctor, dentist, dry cleaners). You could enclose some movie passes or gift certificates for a fun dinner somewhere.

Bring a basket of things they may need right away, like paper towels, toilet paper, Windex, paper plates, trash bags, etc.

Bring over a two-tier turntable and offer to organize (alphabetize) her spices for her while she unpacks.

Ask them where they came from, what brought them to this area, how many children they have, etc.

MY IDEAS:

_____

_____

_____

HOW CAN I SAY NO?

*J*ust because someone asks us to do something doesn't mean we have to do it. Our first responsibility is to our immediate family. Saying yes to things that don't really matter often means saying no to the things that matter most—your family. Don't shortchange them in your efforts to be "nice."

If you agree to do something and end up not doing it because you had too much on your plate, the person you let down will be more unhappy with you than she would have had you said no in the first place. So learn to say no and don't feel guilty about it.

"I would love to be on the decorating committee with you, but the timing is wrong for me. Maybe next year."

"I wish I could drive your carpool for you while you are on vacation next week, but I'm having a tough time meeting my own commitments right now."

"I'm sorry I can't bring a casserole over to Mary anytime this week, I haven't even had time to prepare meals for my own family. We've been eating takeout." (Maybe she'll add you to her list of people who could use a meal now and then).

"I'd love to be on the activities committee, but we've been so busy that we haven't even gone to the last few activities. I wouldn't want to let you down."

If your boss asks you to stay late to finish a project say, "I can't stay late, but I can come in early tomorrow." Or say, "We could finish it sooner if we got someone else to help on the project."

Be honest. Don't make up false excuses. It's far better to simply say "no" and decline than to justify your refusal with a fabricated story.

What (or who) would I love to be able to say no to?

_____

_____

_____

How could I say it?

_____

_____

_____

HOW TO RESPOND WHEN YOUR LOVED ONE OFFENDS YOU

*B*enjamin Franklin said, "Any fool can criticize, condemn, and complain, and most fools do."

The closer we are to people, the less guarded we are in our conversations. Sometimes we speak without thinking about how what we are saying will be perceived.

When a loved one hurts your feelings, assume it was unintended. Be the bigger person. Forgive and forget.

If you have to get it off your chest, say, "I've been thinking about what you said the other day and I'm sure you didn't mean it the way it sounded, but when you said _____ it hurt my feelings." If he offers an apology, accept it. If he doesn't, ask if you have done anything to offend him. If he says no, then he is just an insensitive person. Don't take anything he says personally.

What do I do?

_____

_____

_____

What "should" I do?

_____

_____

_____

HOW TO SHIELD YOUR CHILDREN FROM OFFENSIVE MATERIAL

*O*ffensive material is everywhere in our society. It's impossible to shield your children from all of it. There are steps you can take to limit it. The easiest place to secure is your own home. Take advantage of the computer and TV parental controls. Don't allow your children to use the computer or TV unsupervised (in other words, don't let them have a computer or TV in their bedroom). Make sure the computer or TV is in a popular, open, or busy room in the house. Just knowing that someone could walk by any moment and see what is on the screen is a deterrent. If you happen to be watching TV as a family and see offensive advertising or previews of scary movies, quickly change the channel and comment, "Oh I wish they wouldn't show that trash on TV, I don't want to see that."

Or say, "They must think we are stupid if they think we would respond to that kind of advertising."

If you see an offensive billboard or advertising on passing vehicles or on storefronts, don't call attention to it unless you see your children already looking. If you don't say anything to call their attention to it, they may not notice it. If they do see it, use it as a learning experience about how unfortunate it is that advertisers have to stoop so low to get people's attention. Let them know you strongly disapprove of that kind of advertising, but because we live in a country that allows free speech, sometimes people take advantage of it. Try to avoid bringing children to places where inappropriate material is likely to be prevalent.

The same goes for people wearing offensive clothing. There is no point trying to tell the person they shouldn't be wearing that t-shirt in public where children are exposed to it. They don't care. They are wearing the shirt to make a statement and offend people. Their goal is to be in your face. If you say anything to them you will more than likely be embroiled in an ugly scene, which would be even more offensive to your children.

If your twelve-year-old wants to go to a PG-13 or R-rated movie, tell him you aren't the one who made the rules. If you approve of the movie, you have to go with him. If you don't approve, he has to follow the rules. I've seen parents with young children watching movies that were totally inappropriate for their age. You really ought to think twice before taking children to these movies. They are rated for a reason.

If you end up in a situation where you feel uncomfortable, it is always appropriate to leave.

What can I do to shield my children?

_____

_____

PARENT TEACHER RELATIONSHIPS

*I*t used to be that if a teacher contacted a parent, the teacher was taken seriously and the child held accountable. Not so anymore. Parents believe their child's account of the situation and discount the teacher's accusations.

Children are no longer being taught to respect authority. Somebody needs a wake-up call. Children must be told that the teacher may not always be right, that life isn't always fair and that the good guy doesn't always win.

Parents need to stop fighting their children's battles for them. How will these kids ever get along in the real world? They need to know that the boss may not always be right, but he's always the boss. It's a valuable life lesson.

NOTES:

_____

_____

WHAT DO YOU SAY OR DO WHEN YOUR LOVED ONE HAS EXPERIENCED PHYSICAL ABUSE?

*H*elp her understand that it is not her fault. She will say she provoked him, that she should have known better, etc. Remind her that there is no excuse for this kind of violent behavior.

If she believes that slapping, hitting, punching, and raping are a "man's right" within his home, she is wrong. Nor is it permissible to hit a person to teach them a lesson. Some women don't recognize emotional abuse for what it is. Often a woman may mistakenly think that as long as her husband doesn't hit her, she isn't really being abused. Or she may say, "He hasn't hit me for months." This could be true, however, often when physical abuse decreases emotional abuse increases. A woman doesn't have to put up with being put down.

Don't try to force your friend to move out of the house. It has to be her decision. Tell her, "If you are strong enough to stay, you are strong enough to leave." Give her the telephone number of a shelter near her. (Call 1–800–333-SAFE to find the nearest shelter, call your local YWCA, or call the National Domestic Violence Hotline 1–800–799-SAFE and ask their advice.) By offering your home you may be placing yourself and your family in danger of her partner's rage. Encourage her to report instances of abuse to the police.

Ask questions about the abuser. Is he violent with anyone else besides her? Agree on a codeword that she can use to call you to come to her aid. Read more about code words in Marian Betancourt's book *What to Do When Love Turns Violent*. It might not be a good idea to give your friend the book. She might have difficulty explaining to her abuser why you gave it to her.

If you ever witness verbal abuse in a relationship, including put-downs that undermine self-esteem, tell the person in private that they don't deserve to be treated that way. Don't challenge the abuser in public.

The most important thing you can do is to get both parties into counseling. That is the only long-term solution. If she can't get her husband to go, she should go alone. Offer to take her.

Keep confidences. If your friend asks you not to tell anyone else what she is going through, respect her wishes. She needs to know she can count on you. If you tell, she won't talk to you anymore, and she may have no place else to go.

What would I want someone to do for me if I were in this situation?

_____

_____

_____

_____

WHAT TO DO WHEN YOUR LOVED ONE
ANNOUNCES THAT SHE IS PREGNANT

*R*esist the temptation to rub the pregnant woman's belly. She is not the Buddha. It will not bring you luck.

Also, try to refrain from proffering unsolicited baby advice. Did you have all 6 kids without the aid of any medication? Good for you. Surprisingly, natural birth does not work for everyone. Even many women who intend to give birth naturally, eventually succumb to the need for medication. Similarly, breastfeeding does not always work for everyone. Decisions such as natural birth vs. epidural, breast vs. bottle-feeding, nutrition and weight gain are ultimately between the woman and her health practitioner. There are enough feelings of guilt and inadequacy attendant with motherhood without the misguided "helpful advice" from strangers and acquaintances. Unless the pregnant woman is a very close friend and you are sure that your "help" will be taken in the right spirit, keep you opinions to yourself.

The same thing goes for baby names. Perhaps there is a sense of pride and personal satisfaction derived from providing a pregnant couple with the "winning" baby name. Nevertheless, do not start offering an onslaught of suggestions. Unless a couple is specifically asking for naming advice, the never-ending barrage of name suggestions (from everyone from the local grocer to aunt Edna's best friend) is often more daunting than a determining factor in the final decision. This is especially true if the couple has already narrowed down the options to a select few. Do you despise one of the alternatives? Regardless of how intimate your relationship with the couple (grandparents of the baby-to-be take note), *lie!* Don't rob the couple of the joy they have found upon the name they have selected. It was a lengthy selection process and was not made in haste. Do you consider Molly a cow's name? Is Waverly reserved for prostitutes? Whatever your personal connotation and/or association with a couple's dream name, fight the urge to intervene. Lie through your teeth and tell the beaming parents that it is absolutely adorable and the perfect name for their future bundle of joy. Chances are, no matter how much you may hate the idea of a little girl named Kennedy, five months after she's born you will be unable to picture her as anything else.

New mothers need a little extra support in the beginning. It takes a while to adjust to a newborn's schedule. If your friend's mother is not around to help out at this crucial time, you might stop by every other day or so and offer to hold the baby while she takes a shower and gets dressed for the day. Or you can offer to either run some errands for her or babysit while she runs errands, buys groceries, etc. She might like some help getting the baby to his first and second doctor appointments.

NOTES:

_____

_____

_____

WHAT TO DO WHEN YOUR LOVED ONE GETS A PROMOTION

*H*urray, something to celebrate. In this world where everything seems to be going downhill, it is nice to see your loved ones being rewarded for their hard work. Make it a celebration. Have some people over and make the announcement. Take your loved one out to dinner or make a special dinner at home.

Find a card that expresses your feelings. Send helium balloons. Express your appreciation for how hard he (or she) has worked to earn this recognition and how proud you are of their accomplishment.

What I would do:

_____

_____

HOW DO YOU RESPOND WHEN SOMEONE ASKS INAPPROPRIATE QUESTIONS?

"Wow, you have a nice house. How much did you pay for it?"

"More than I planned on."

"You don't want to know."

"How much money does your husband make a year?"

"Half as much as I wish he did."

"How old are you?"

"Can you keep a secret? So can I."

If the person continues to repeat his question, you can say, "You can keep asking, but you will keep getting the same answer." Some people just don't, or won't, quit. If that is the case, you just might have to be blunt. "My husband and I make it a practice not to discuss our finances [personal business, whatever]."

What I would say:

_____

_____

YOUR CHILD IS INVITED TO A BIRTHDAY PARTY WHERE THEY WILL BE SHOWING AN INAPPROPRIATE MOVIE

*I*f your child is younger than eight years old, you should call the mother and tell her that your child would love to go, but that you feel your child is not ready to handle that particular movie. Ask when she planned to show the movie and if it is at the end of the party, you could have your child attend the party, then pick him up early.

If your child is eight or older, he should handle the situation himself. He should talk to the birthday boy himself. If he is uncomfortable saying that he doesn't want to watch the movie, he can say that his mother doesn't want him to see that particular movie and he has to respect her wishes.

Sometimes the parent can explain the problem to the child and let it be his decision whether to attend or not. Kids need practice in using their free agency. If he has nightmares because of the movie, he will learn something about consequences of choices.

(If you are not willing to accept whatever decision he makes, you're not ready to let him make the decisions yet.)

Sometimes when people are aware that the movie is a problem, they are willing to change the movie or make special arrangements to accommodate the child.

When my daughters were in high school, they were put in situations where the teacher planned to show an R-rated movie. When they told the teacher that they thought the movie was inappropriate, the teacher gave them an assignment to work on in the library during the showing of the movie.

What I think:

_____

_____

HOW TO RESPOND TO RELIGIOUS CEREMONIES AND ORDINANCES

*R*egardless of your own religious beliefs, it's important to recognize the momentous events of your friends of other faiths. If you have been invited to attend a religious ceremony, it is because your friend recognizes it as an important event. Be supportive. Extend the same excitement and attention as you would to a member of your own faith or an equally important occasion. Don't stay away just because you don't understand the event. Ask your friend questions. Find out if there are any dos and don'ts you need to be aware of. Your friend's explanation of the ceremony will give you an indication of the importance of the event.

Show them the same respect for their beliefs you would hope to be shown in return.

Baptisms, bar mitzvahs, christenings, communions, etc., are all important events that you may be invited to.

"Congratulations! I'm so happy for you" works for almost any occasion.

If you would like to attend, express your desire. If you would like to give them a gift to remember the day, do so. An appropriate gift might be something that could be engraved with the date (a crystal paperweight, a silver frame, a brass bookmark).

Friends of mine who belong to other faiths are:

Name	Their Religion

NOTES:

HOW TO TALK TO YOUR CHILDREN ABOUT SEX, DRUGS, AND OTHER UNCOMFORTABLE SUBJECTS

*K*ids who feel they can talk with their parents about sex or drugs are less likely to engage in high-risk behavior as teens than kids who do not feel they can talk with their parents about the subject.

How do you start the conversation? Say something like, "You know, I'm uncomfortable talking about sex and drugs because my parents never talked with me about it. But I want us to be able to talk about anything—sex, drugs, or whatever else is on your mind—so please come to me if you have any questions. I'd rather you get your information from me than from your peers, who may or may not know what they're talking about."

The earlier you start the better. I used to use the time spent driving my kids around as good conversation opportunities. I always asked them what they wanted to talk about and invariably it was sex or drugs.

Give age appropriate information. When a six-year-old asks where babies come from, you don't need to go into the whole discussion of sex. A simple explanation will suffice. As they grow older, you can give more information. You know your child and what kind of information is best for him or her.

There are excellent books to help you explain these questions to your five or six-year old.

Try *Where Did I Come From?* by Peter Mayle, Arthur Robins, and Paul Walter or

What's the Big Secret? by Lauren Krasny Brown and Marc Brown.

If a girl is eight or nine, she is ready for more information. You might include the process of menstruation, which is something that will happen to her in the not-too-distant future, and what she should do when it happens. A neighbor friend of mine when I was growing up had no clue why she started bleeding. She thought she was going to bleed to death. It is better to get this information too soon, than too late.

Here are two suggestions for books to help explain menstruation: *Period: A Girl's Guide* by JoAnn Loulan, Bonnie Worthen or *Tilly's Birthday: A Young Girl's Introduction to Menstruation* by Lorell Gordon. Check your local bookstore or amazon.com for more books on this topic or anything else you'd like to discuss with your children.

Talking about drugs and alcohol needs to start earlier than one would expect. It is not unusual for eleven-year-olds to start drinking alcohol. You need to be on top of this one.

Is your medicine cabinet filled with prescription medicine? Don't take your pills in front of your kids. If they do see you, explain to them what the pill is for and that your doctor told you to take it. Emphasize that they should *never* take any one else's pills, for *any* reason. Their friends may tell them it's cool to take a bunch of pills and see what happens. But a mix of pills that you don't know anything about are more likely to stop your heart than to give you a high.

When they ask why people take drugs, you can say, "Maybe they don't know how dangerous they are," or "Maybe they feel bad about themselves or don't know how to handle their problems," or "Maybe they don't have parents they can talk to. Why do you think they do it?"

We may think our kids are too young for these discussions, but our kids are already hearing about these issues from TV, movies, magazines, and school friends. If we don't talk with them and answer their questions, they'll get their facts from someone else. And we'll have missed an opportunity to offer information that's not only accurate, but also goes along with our own personal values and moral principles.

NOTES:

_____

_____

HOW TO SAY "I'M SORRY"

*L*ove is never having to say you're sorry, right? Wrong. No matter how much you love a person, from time to time you are going to hurt their feelings. It doesn't matter whether or not you think they have a legitimate complaint, the fact remains that their feelings are hurt. You can't argue with that. What you have to do is apologize—sincerely. You didn't mean to hurt their feelings—say so.

"I would never say anything to hurt your feelings. I'm so sorry."

We don't know everything that is going on in another person's life. Sometimes we may say something, inadvertently, that hits a nerve. They may take something we say the wrong way and think we are saying something entirely different. Regardless, use "I" phrases, not "you" phrases. Saying "you misunderstood" or "you took it wrong" places the mistake with the other party. It is more of an accusation than an apology. Instead say, "I am so sorry I hurt you. I never meant it that way. Please forgive me."

When you are at fault, admit it. Be specific. Don't simply say "sorry." Put yourself in the other person's place and apologize specifically for the hurt or damage you may have caused.

Don't offer an empty or insincere apology simply to end the conversation. Even if you don't think you're in the wrong, you can still apologize for hurting the person's feelings.

Is there anyone I need to apologize to?

NOTES:

_____

_____

HOW TO SUPPORT A FRIEND WHO IS ASPIRING TO ACHIEVE SUCCESS IN A FIELD WHERE HE/SHE LACKS THE TALENT TO SUCCEED

*Y*our friend thinks he's the next American Idol, but he sounds more like William Hung. Do you tell him to pursue his dream, or do you tell him not to quit his day job?

Many of the pitiable A.I. contestants in the audition shows truly believe they have a special talent. Typically, these people have little else going for them in their lives and base their self-worth upon this perceived skill. There is no reason to take that away from them. Feed the fantasy and be full of praise.

If your friend is wasting his life in the pursuit of pipe dreams, you may have to intercede. For the college grad who wishes to pursue a career in a field in which he lacks the skill to succeed, you might suggest that he put a time limit on his dream. If he has not been offered a football contract (record deal, signed with a modeling agency, etc.) after one year, suggest he return to pursuing more practical goals. For the middle-aged man, his choices might affect his wife and kids, those who rely on him for support. Unless he has a very probable channel for success, you may need to dissuade him from jeopardizing the stability of his home. Suggest he pursue his talent as a hobby. He can get involved in a local theater production, organize weekly sporting events (like football Friday nights, tennis Tuesdays, etc.), or form a band and arrange to play in local venues. If he is adamant, suggest he wait until he has a contract before he quit his "day job." It is important to be able to give our goals a legitimate chance, but we cannot live the remainder of our lives dreaming. At a certain point, we must accept the reality of our limitations and focus on something we can achieve success pursuing.

If a person has the financial resources available to pursue their dreams without any detriment to themselves or their families, be supportive. Many people are bored with their lives and are seeking diversion in an industry full of fame, glory, or financial success. For others, pursuing a career in the entertainment industry has always been a dream. Support your friend, tell him you think he's really good, but there is a *lot* of competition out there and not to think less of himself if he can't achieve his goal. It is not just talent that propels a person to stardom. I've seen a lot of really talented singers and actors who are much better than most pop stars and actors, but they just weren't at the right place at the right time. No matter how talented you are, a person needs a lot of luck, timing, and making the right connections.

NOTES:

_____

_____

WHAT TO DO WHEN YOUR LOVED ONE IS DEALING WITH TEEN PREGNANCY

*T*his is the nightmare of every parent of a teenage daughter. There is no "good" solution.

There are four options:

1. The most obvious is for the two to marry. (However, ninety percent will be divorced within six years).

2. Give the baby up for adoption. (This is the best option for the baby, but difficult for most families to accept).

3. Keep the baby. (Ninety percent keep the baby. However, this is usually not the best option for the child).

4. Abort the baby. (One out of five pregnancies end in abortion).

What You Can Do

Be a friend.

Support whatever decision she makes (after considering all the alternatives carefully). Avoid subjecting her to your personal religious beliefs or to the tales of people you know and their choices. Each situation is different and what works for one family may not work for another. Again, the most important question is what will be best for the baby, and then, what is best for the young woman.

Don't moralize or be judgmental.

Listen. Let her express her concerns, fears, regrets, etc.

Don't dwell on the past. Once the decision is made, go forward and help her make the best life she can for herself.

What would I want someone to do for me if I were in this situation?

_____

_____

NOTES:

_____

_____

HOW TO DEAL WITH TELEMARKETERS

*T*here is nothing more annoying that just sitting down to dinner, or your favorite TV show, and having the phone ring. Oh wait, there is something more annoying: the person calling you is a telemarketer.

As frustrating as these interruptions might be, do not take your hostility out on the poor student on the other end of the line. Telemarketers are typically college students or people otherwise desperate for employment. They are not out to make your life miserable—it's just a job. Refrain from using rudeness or profanities, but politely explain that you are not interested. There is no need to hang up on the person. Civilly say "goodbye" and you might even wish them well. Treat them in the same way you would hope people would treat your own son or daughter if they were similarly employed.

You have probably already heard of the National Do Not Call list, but you may not know how to get your telephone number on it. Here it is. You can register your phone number for free, and it will remain on the national do-not-call list for five years. You must call from the phone you wish to register. The number to call is 1–888–382–1222.

You can also register online at www.donotcall.gov.

Registering won't stop every annoying call. Charitable and political organizations are exempt from the list. You don't need to register your cell phone, despite the emails that have been circulating to the contrary.

Sorry, there is no national "Do not knock on my door" registry. So when you get knocks on your door, you have to peek through your curtains like you've always done and choose to answer or not.

Keep in mind that all the religious missionaries sincerely believe in what they are doing and want to share the knowledge they have with you. They are sacrificing other things they could be doing in order to share their message with you. Don't be rude to them.

If you already belong to another church, politely tell them so. If you don't belong to any particular church and are interested in hearing what they have to say, give them a chance, but if in the end it still isn't for you, tell them. If you act like you are at all interested, they'll be back. You'll just be wasting your time and theirs.

Expect to be hit up by all the neighborhood kids selling Girl Scout cookies, magazines, and wrapping paper. There is only so much of this stuff you can store. If you don't want to participate, just tell them someone else beat them to your door and you've already participated. If you want to help the kids, but can't use all the "stuff," donate it to local charities. (Or you could save the cookies and give them to the kids selling magazines.)

HOW IS YOUR TELEPHONE ETIQUETTE?

Sometimes we are in such a hurry to get our message across that we forget the pleasantries of telephone conversations. We need to first ask if we are calling at a convenient time. Your friend may be in the middle of dinner or in the middle of a family crisis. There could have been an accident or death in the family. Always give the person an opportunity to call you back at a more convenient time for them.

In this age of cell phones and caller ID, some people assume that the person on the other end knows the identity of the caller before they even pick up the phone. This is not always the case. I once saw an acquaintance who had been talking on the phone for nearly twenty minutes suddenly state, "Julie. Julie Jenkins!" Don't assume that the person on the other end automatically knows it's you. Very few acquaintances are intimate enough to say simply, "It's me."

People can hear when you are smiling. The reverse is also true. There is never any cause to be curt or abrupt when someone calls you. If it is not a convenient time to talk, politely tell the caller so. You cannot choose when a call will come, but you can always choose whether or not to answer it. It is not the fault of the person on the other end if they called during your favorite TV show or during a heated discussion with your spouse.

Who is doing all the talking? If you are, take a breather and give the other person a chance to talk.

Don't just call people when you want something from them. Call occasionally just to chat and see what's going on in their life.

When you ask about her children, call them by name not just, "What are the kids up to?" Ask specific questions like, "What colleges is Aaron applying to?" or "Is Shelly still taking dance lessons?"

If your friend has been on vacation, call her and ask how the vacation went. What was her favorite place? Were the hotels nice? How was the food, weather, etc.? Show your interest in her life.

Even if you call at a convenient time, that doesn't mean you can impose on their time.

If you can't say what you need to say in thirty minutes, you need to meet for lunch. Some people *love* talking on the phone and could do so for hours. Most people are not that way. If you fall into the former category, try to be courteous of your friend's time. If you are calling just to chat, give you friend the option to resume the conversation at a later time. If you are the friend who does not like the hour-long chats, sometimes it is best to be the caller. This way, the length of the call is more in your control. Moreover, you can call your friend at a more convenient time for you and even block out a half hour if you know it will be a long call.

If you frequently call someone and somebody else answers, and then there is a long pause followed by an excuse why the person you called is unavailable, you might want to think about why they are avoiding you. You either need to sharpen your telephone skills or find yourself another friend.

How is my telephone etiquette? What do I need to work on?

_____

_____

WHAT TO DO FOR A LOVED ONE WHO IS DIAGNOSED WITH A TERMINAL ILLNESS

*E*arly on in this process, people typically enter a state of denial, pretending there has been a huge mistake. If your friend is in this category, it's okay to go along with his assessment of his condition. Let him be optimistic. As time passes, his view of the situation will change and you can get your cues from his behavior and from how he talks about his illness.

When you greet your friend, ask him how he is doing. He will most likely answer, "Fine," or something like that. Don't be afraid to press the issue, "No, I mean really. How are you?" Often times people want to talk about their problems, but are hesitant to burden others.

Don't avoid your friend or family member because you don't know what to say. Just go for a short visit and let the other do the talking, or go with someone else—but go.

Don't worry about what to say. Focus on your love of the person. He will feel it. Just say, "It's good to see you. I've missed you." Say, "I'm here for you." Then be there. Listen. Let him talk about his fears. Encourage him to make plans for his death but remind him that he is alive now and to enjoy each day he has.

Tell him he looks great, considering what he is going through. Tell him how well he is handling his situation. Tell him how many people are asking about him. Don't tell him he looks great, however, if he looks dreadful. You'll lose all credibility.

If he has been, or is going to be, in the hospital for a long time and has children, take photos of the kids and bring them to him. Help link him to the outside world. Talk about what's going on in the world, with you and your family, etc. Decorate his hospital room for holidays.

Don't be afraid to say the name of his illness. You don't have to avoid the subject.

When first diagnosed with a terminal illness, the person needs to re-evaluate his life. Encourage him to focus on what's really important. Laugh more, love more, play more. Enjoy today. In the beginning, don't give up hope no matter what the odds. The truth of the matter is that no doctor knows how long any patient will live. Miracles happen. A medical break through could come any day. Try to be positive, not negative. But it is unkind to give false hope. Sooner or later the person must face reality.

Make it as easy as possible for your friend to say what he or she has to say. If you end up crying together, don't feel that you've failed. It was what was needed.

Don't feel like you have to always be talking. It's okay to have some quiet time. Watching TV together can relieve the pressure of conversation. Tell the person to feel free to rest and take a nap if they are so inclined. It can be exhausting sometimes to have visitors that demand your full attention.

Tell him he is in your prayers.

Ask if there is anyone in particular he would like to see and bring that person by.

Bring him stationery to write notes if he is able, and if not, have him dictate notes to you to send to his friends.

Books on tape make a nice gift and a small tape player if none are available.

Co-workers can take photos of the office workers and make a scrapbook or frame a photo of the whole group.

Friends can get together and plan a fundraiser if there are financial needs in the family.

If the person has been, or will be hospitalized for a long period of time, someone could make a video: places the person liked to go, his or her hometown, friends' personal greetings, etc.

What would I want someone to do for me if I were terminally ill?

_____

_____

_____

NOTES:

_____

_____

_____

HOW TO AVOID TRAVEL FAUX PAS OR HOW TO AVOID BEING AN "UGLY AMERICAN"

*F*irst and foremost, learn the language, or at least make some effort. When it comes to foreign dialects, a little effort goes a long way. Do not immediately start speaking English and assume that the native should understand you. Always attempt to converse with the locals in their own language first. If nothing else, learn basics such as "please," "thank you," "how much," and "good morning/night." Often, locals will be more willing to converse in English when they see you making an effort.

Many foreigners complain that Americans are loud. Increasing the volume of your voice will not help locals to understand your English any better. Instead, if you are speaking English, speak slowly and clearly. When in groups, be cognizant of your surroundings. Churches, temples, and other holy places should be approached with reverence and respect.

Be patient. You are not the only one who traveled thousands of miles to see the Eiffel Tower (as is evidenced by the innumerable masses lined up at its base). Don't be rude or pushy. Smile. Be friendly and kind.

Learn local customs and try to observe local mores. Be respectful of the culture you are entering. Don't call attention to yourself. Blend in.

Before you go, inquire into dress restrictions, dietary codes, local customs, etc. Don't order bacon in a Jewish restaurant. Don't wear shorts or tank tops to the Vatican. A helpful tip: travel with a shawl or pareo in your handbag that can be wrapped around your shoulders or waist if the dress code requires it. (This can be applicable anywhere from Rome to Thailand.)

Don't criticize local customs or citizenry. The mid-day siesta is not evidence of a "lazy" workforce. The topless women on the beach are not lewd or morally corrupt. Do not judge others based upon your own country's code of conduct. Most other societies run at a much slower pace than we do. Don't complain about the slow service; it's the way they do business. You are on vacation. Also bear in mind that in many countries, the bill is not brought to the table until it is requested. It is considered rude to interrupt a person's leisurely meal by bringing the check. Again, be aware of local customs.

Be willing to try new foods and pretend to like it. If you are eating in a person's home, be aware of what is expected. In some countries it is rude to decline second, third, or even fourth servings. I was once accused of disliking a woman's cooking because I refused a fourth helping of her spaghetti. In countries where such is the custom, take several *small* helpings of food so that you can request another serving with frequency.

Most countries practice the art of "negotiation" when it comes to purchasing souvenirs, etc. During this process, avoid making disparaging remarks about the merchandise or the salesperson. So what if you overpay a little? If you can afford to travel, you can afford to pay a fair price (consider the excess a charitable donation).

When you are a part of a tour group, it is especially critical to be on your best behavior. Nothing stands out more than a horde of rude Americans loudly complaining and pushing their way through a crowd. Be mindful and respectful of those around you. Be courteous.

I was traveling with a tour group through Mexico and was impressed with one particular couple. When the bus stopped for us to buy souvenirs, some local children were gathering to watch us. The couple rounded up the kids and taught them how to play "duck, duck, goose." The children's parents started coming out to see what was going on and they loved it. I'm sure they talked about this particular tour group for some time after the event.

On another occasion, while traveling through Africa, one couple brought things from home to pass out to children. We stopped at a small village and they passed out bubble gum, pencils, and pens.

If you will be a guest in someone's home during your visit, it would be thoughtful of you to bring a gift (perhaps a coffee table book of your state, a cookbook of typical American food, or some other typically American item that would easily fit in your suitcase).

Other customs to be aware of: removing shoes, types of greetings (kisses, bowing, etc).

Remember, you are in a position to make a permanent impression of what Americans are like. Be a good example.

NOTES:

_____

_____

YOUR LOVED ONE IS DEALING WITH UNEMPLOYMENT

*L*ike other losses, being fired or laid off can cause a grief reaction. In addition to anger and despair, the person faces loss of self-esteem and sense of purpose, coupled with feelings of shame and financial hardship.

Your loved one needs to know that 25 percent of the population will slip into poverty at one time or another. So he is not alone or worthless. He needs to know that this is only temporary.

Encourage him to talk about his situation. Networking is an important factor in finding work.

Encourage him to keep on sending out resumes even when discouraged. Don't give up.

To give up is to lose out.

Tell your friend that it is okay to take a cut in pay. It is better than remaining unemployed.

Be sensitive to their lack of finances. Don't ask them to participate in things that cost money. Bring dinners in for the family. Offer to run errands, take kids to school, pick up groceries, etc. to conserve gas. Pass along your newspapers, magazines, etc.

If you notice that their children are being left out of things that cost money (field trips, sports activities, etc.) offer to pay their way if you can afford to. (It is better to go directly to the teacher or coach and have him tell the family that there is no cost for their child. Often the family is too proud to accept money from others.)

What would I want someone to do for me if I were unemployed?

_____

_____

_____

_____

HOW TO HANDLE A WAYWARD TEEN?

T asked the mother of a wayward child what was the worst advice she ever got. Her answer was, "He'll grow out of it." I was shocked. I would have thought that would be the most comforting thing you could say. Her response was that the problem with that attitude is that while you are waiting for him to grow out of it, you are doing nothing to change the situation. You are waiting for him, who is wrong, to realize that you and your values are right. You need to be in constant communication. You need to tell him that although you disapprove of the choices he has made, you still love him. When he comes to you to bail him out of his problems, you need to lovingly tell him that the problem he is dealing with is the consequence of the choices he has made. Make him deal with it.

If you have a friend that is hurting because she has what she considers to be a "wayward child," you might have a conversation with her and bring up some of the following thoughts.

Things don't always turn out the way we planned, regardless of how many little league games we attended, hours we spent in the car taking our children to scouts, dance classes, and the myriad of activities we supported over the years.

What happened? How did that adorable obedient child of yours turn into this stranger? You want to shake him and say, "Who are you and what have you done with my child!"

But remember, what to you may be an errant child, may not be to someone else. Someone else may think you are crazy to be upset over that type of "transgression."

Is he a juvenile delinquent? Is he on drugs? Is he gay? Has he turned his back on your religious beliefs and/or moral convictions? Does he have purple hair, tattoos, and a dozen body pierces? Is he a grown son who is still irresponsible and unable to provide for himself or his family? Has he abused his wife or children? Is he in jail? When people ask about him are you embarrassed to talk about him?

According to the Bureau of Justice statistics, there were over 15 million arrests in the year 1995 alone. That's 15 million mothers worried about their kids. There were also 1,080,728 people in state and federal prisons. In 1995 there were 513,486 reported cases of AIDS and there are anywhere from 2 to 3 million people estimated to have HIV. There are 4 million women being abused by their husbands. There are from 6 to 9 million out of work every year and 2.7 million teenage girls get pregnant every year. Who knows how many are in gangs? The list goes on and on. They all have mothers who worry.

What can a person do when embarrassed by children's behavior and choices in life? If you or a friend is in this dilemma, what can you do?

What You Can Do

First, the parent must quit taking responsibility for the child's behavior. The child made the choices, and he has to suffer the consequences of his behavior.

I've known many preachers' sons who were wayward children. Was the preacher to blame? In each case there were several children in the family. Only one was a problem. All the children were raised with the same values.

Only one chose to ignore them. Are you any smarter than a man of God? What makes you think you could raise perfect children?

One explanation for the difference in kids all raised in the same family with the same rules could be the role of the "non-shared environment." It is who influences their behavior outside of the home setting. Who are your children's role models? Every child has one. Is the child influenced by a favorite teacher or by a violent, out-of-control super athlete? Do you know who your child's friends are? How well do you know them?

Young people need worthy goals. Help your child develop a plan.

Parents should be aware of early warning signs and take them seriously. Early professional intervention can alter behavior. The longer the behavior is permitted the less likely change will occur.

Your best hope for the future is the old saying that the fruit doesn't fall far from the tree. If he is a young man, there is still plenty of time for him to realize the error of his ways and return to the principles you have taught him.

It is natural for children to try to do things their way. Children, especially young adults, want to assert their independence. They will find out the value of the principles you have taught them and return to them, one by one.

Be patient. Have faith. Don't widen the gap and make it more difficult for them to return. Let them know that you love them. It is their behavior that you can't tolerate.

Don't get hung up on unimportant things. Be selective in what you choose to do battle over. Make a list of all the things that bother you. Then rank them. Go after the top priority items and drop the bottom half of the list. Resolve not to bring up any of those issues.

If they are underage and doing things you don't approve of, should you throw them out of the house? (There are 1.3 million runaways, most are homeless living on the streets. Most runaways return within 48 hours. See chapter on kidnapping for what to do if your child runs away and call Covenant House 1–800–999–9999. They will give you a list of things to do to find your teen.)

Ask Yourself These Questions

If I throw him out, where will he go? Will I be throwing him into the very environment I'm trying to keep him out of? (Isn't he safer at home where you can keep an eye on him and know of his comings and goings?) One of my favorite sayings is, "The best way to keep teenagers home is to make their surroundings pleasant—and let the air out of the tires." Seriously, take away his car keys.

Is he a bad influence on siblings? Will they follow his lead? (Usually not. They see the heartbreak you are feeling and don't want to add to it. Especially if you are praising them for their good behavior.)

Is he a "danger" to siblings? Is he violent? If he poses a real threat to the family, he needs to be removed. Not thrown out in the street, but put in a facility that can care for him.

If he is over 18, don't "fund" his behavior. By allowing him to live at home and giving him money when he needs it you are an "enabler." Tell him as long as he is living under your roof and getting money from you

WHAT *to say* and do WHEN . . .

he has to live by the Golden Rule: "He who has the gold makes the rules." If he is not willing, he should move out and support himself.

College Students and Drugs

Make a deal with your graduating senior. You will pay for college if he stays off drugs. How will you know?

1. If he gets "busted," that's the end of your support.

2. You know he is capable of maintaining a "B" average. He couldn't have gotten into college if he weren't, so, if his grade point falls below what he's capable of doing, consider it a red flag. If he wants to continue college, he has to fund it. If he wants an education, he'll get it. If he doesn't care, you are wasting your money and he'd be taking up space that could be filled by someone else who does care. It's his life now.

If he has graduated from high school and is still living at home, ask him to move out. Help him find a job, pay his first month's rent, and tell him he is now on his own. He is welcome to come back home if and when he is willing to live by your standards. As long as he wants to do his own thing, let him do it—in his own place, with his own money. Don't make it a screaming match.

Here's a scenario: Your son has been drinking and doing drugs. He doesn't honor any curfew. He comes and goes as he pleases, sometimes not coming home at all for several days. And yet, he still asks you for money (clothes, gas, food, etc.). You and your husband should sit him down:

"Johnny, your father and I have had a long talk about you and we have decided that it's time you move on with your life. You are no longer a child and shouldn't have to be treated like one. You need to make your own decisions and learn how to get by in life on your own. We think that time has come. It will be hard for you at first, but we feel you are ready. We want you to get a job (we'll help you find one if you want) and find a place you can afford. We'll pay your first month's rent. Then you are on your own. Don't come to us for money; that defeats the whole purpose. You need to learn how to manage your money." All this is done without yelling or name-calling.

When your child moves out, be sure to show your love and concern for his welfare by calling him, sending him notes (and occasional care packages), and inviting him to dinner.

Treat your children as if they already are what you hope them to be, and they will become such.

NOTES:

_____

_____

WHAT TO SAY TO A BRIDE'S SINGLE FRIENDS AT A WEDDING

*A*s surprising as this may sound, not all women sit at bridal showers and weddings dreaming of their own. They do not need consolation and encouragement that this will one day happen for them. They do not need the admonition to "hurry up" or "get on it" themselves. A woman who is single, divorced, or widowed often feels uncomfortable in groups that consist of couples and families. Make it as comfortable as possible for her.

Don't push her to catch the bouquet, especially if the next oldest girl in the circle is the bride's twelve-year-old niece. Do ask her to dance, sit at your table, talk about the delicious desserts, or offer to get her a drink or food.

For those women who do desperately want to get married and are unable to do so, sometimes the very worst thing is for a well-meaning acquaintance to point out the individual's failure in that department. Unless you are a close personal friend of the woman and she has confided her feelings on the subject, don't offer consolation or advice. There is nothing worse than feeling like the subject of mass speculation and pity. The woman does not want to feel as though everyone at the wedding is talking about her single existence. Sometimes a single woman is perfectly happy at a wedding until a fellow guest starts inquiring about her lack of prospects. Unless the woman is an intimate acquaintance or *she* brings up the subject, leave it alone.

What I would say:

_____

_____

WHAT SHOULD YOU SAY WHEN YOUR LOVED ONE CRITICIZES YOUR WEIGHT?

*T*hrow them off guard. Say something like, "Inside me lives a skinny woman crying to get out. But I can usually shut her up with cookies." It truly amazes me that people think they are "helping" you when they tell you that you are too fat or too thin. Do they really think you don't know? Do they think you've never tried to do anything about it? Do they think you don't know the health risks?

Anorexics may need some intervention, but a doctor is the one to help. Obesity is a huge problem in America (pardon the pun). Being fifty pounds overweight is normal today. (I wanted a gastric bypass to lose my fifty pounds, but my doctor said he doesn't perform them unless the patient is at least 100 pounds overweight). I've tried every diet and lost seventeen pounds (twice) but two years later I was right back where I started from.

The good news is that the extra weight we carry puts pressure on our bones, which helps prevent osteoporosis. (Do I sound like I'm rationalizing? Okay, maybe I am just a little bit. What do I know?)

Be like me, when someone tells me I need to lose some weight, I say, "I know, I'm on a diet right now." Then I follow with, "I'm on a sea food diet. Whenever I see food, I eat it." The truth is, it took me twenty-five years to gain this weight (two pounds a year). My goal now is to take it off the same way—two pounds a year. (By the time I'm eighty, I'll be looking really good.)

How would I handle this?

_____

_____

HOW TO TALK TO PEOPLE IN WHEELCHAIRS

*T*he most important way to interact with a person in a wheelchair is to look them in the eye. Don't ignore people in wheelchairs. Looking over their head or pretending not to see them is rude. That doesn't mean you have to talk to them. If you are not in the habit of talking to strangers, don't stop and talk to them. Treat them like you would treat anyone else.

If you are standing in line and you usually chat with people in line, chat. Few people are offended by an attempt to be friendly. Acknowledging a person with a smile or a few kind words is almost always acceptable (for people in wheelchairs and without!).

If they look like they are having a hard time with the chair, you can offer to assist with a door or curb. You can say something like, "How long have you been in the chair?" If they want to talk about it they will. If not, you'll get the idea and you should back off.

If they are alone and getting around well, they've probably been in a wheelchair a long time and don't need much assistance.

If you see a person in a wheelchair with a silly hat on or with a dog, then that is usually an indication that they want to talk to people. They are giving you a clue that they are approachable. Go ahead, ask them what kind of dog it is, where they got that silly hat, etc. (Caution: the "silly hat" may not be intended as such. There is always the possibility that the hat was not intended to be a conversation starter and the person just has odd taste.)

What would I be comfortable saying?

_____

_____

NOTES:

_____

_____

YOUR LOVED ONE GETS AN UNEXPECTED WINDFALL

*Y*our friend was on the *Price is Right* and she won the showcase, which happened to be two mink coats, two diamond rings, and two cars. Your neighbor just won the lottery. Someone at work just inherited a huge amount of money.

Our first thought when a friend gets an unexpected windfall will surely be, "Why her? Why not me? I need it more than she does." But we are all smart enough to know not to say that out loud.

A true friend is not only there for you in times of hardship and sorrow, but should be there for you clapping and cheering for your accomplishments and good fortune.

"I'm so happy for you."

"Congratulations! It couldn't have happened to a better person."

You know your friend's secret desires: "Now you can . . ."

What ever you do, *don't* ask for a loan, or start making suggestions of how to spend or invest the money.

P.S. I'll tell you a little secret. Nothing is ever what it seems. There is a rule of nature at play in everything. For every good thing that happens, there is a downside and for every bad thing that happens there is a good side. What could possibly be bad about winning two cars, two mink coats, and two diamond rings? Taxes. Your friend can't use all those things, so she will try to sell them. She won't even get half of what they are worth. But she will have to pay tax on the full value of the goods received. She may end up losing and do **WHEN . . .**

ʒo ahead and celebrate with your friend. Before the year is out,
likely be crying on your shoulder.

ʋuld say and do:

_____

_____

CONCLUSION

When your loved one is going through hard times encourage her to focus on what she is grateful for: a roof over her head, her children, health, etc. Have her tape a photo of her kids on her bathroom mirror with a sticky note saying, "Focus on this."

During the good times of your life, create memories. Nothing and no one can ever take that away from you and your family.

The bottom line of this whole book is:

Be yourself—but nicer.

The End?

No, this is just the beginning of the rest of your life.

From this day forward, fill it with love.

:)

For anything not listed in this book, or for more information, go to my website:

Helpingothers.ws

Silverleaf Press Books are available exclusively
in the United States and Canada
through Independent Publishers Group.

For details write or telephone
Independent Publishers Group, 814 North Franklin St.
Chicago, IL 60610, (312) 337-0747

Silverleaf Press
8160 South Highland Drive
Sandy, Utah 84093